I0492935

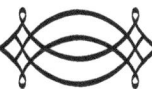

A Journey Through

THE EYES OF AN ORIGINAL HIGHWAYMEN ARTIST

R.L. LEWIS, JR.

As presented by
ROBERT LEWIS, III
ARTWORK BY R.L. LEWIS, JR.

Copyright © 2015 R.L. Lewis, III
ISBN 978-0-9905031-8-7

All Rights Reserved

No part of this book may be reproduced or transmitted in any form or by any means, electronically or mechanically, including photocopying, recording or by an information storage and retrieval system without permission in writing from the author of this book.

Artwork: R.L. Lewis, Jr.

Interior & cover layout & design:
Tarsha L. Campbell

Published by:
DOMINIONHOUSE
Publishing & Design
P.O. Box 681938 | Orlando, Florida 32868 | 407.703.4800
www.mydominionhouse.com

DEDICATION

This book is dedicated to my beloved wife and oldest son, Robert L. Lewis III. They have supported me throughout my artistic adventures! I also salute all of those patrons who purchased my artwork --- blessings to you all.

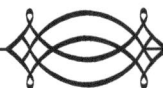

ACKNOWLEDGMENTS

I salute all of the students that I taught at the public

school level, as well as those adults that I taught.

I am especially proud of those students

who pursued art as a career.

Remember to share your gift with others!

Table of Contents

Table of Contents

Featured Artwork

Table of Contents

Featured Artwork

Table of Contents

Featured Artwork

INTRODUCTION

For the Record

Highwaymen is the nickname given to black Florida landscape painters from the early 1950s, 1960s, and early 1970s. History will favorably compare the Highwaymen class of artist to that of the famed Hudson River school of artist. The nickname, "Highwaymen," was coined by the famed art collector Jim Fitch, in 1995. A core group of collectors helped to appraise the art and subsequently identify it for its colorful and unique impressionist Florida landscapes. There are 26 original Florida highwaymen artists—all of which were inducted into the Florida Artist Hall of Fame on March 24, 2004. The term "Highwaymen" was the impetus for helping to put the art into its renaissance mode. This name gave an identifiable name to the art that had been before the public since the early 1950's.

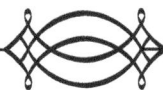

"The personality of the R. L. Lewis I have gotten to know is one of a very humble, generous man with an easy smile and immense sense of humor. He engages in conversations with people as if he has all day to laugh and tell stories."

R.L. LEWIS – FOREWORD

There are some lights in this world that should never grow dim. The brilliant talents of R. L. Lewis, Jr., are to be appreciated, studied, and savored. This book provides a glimpse into his life and his works.

I grew up in south Florida in the '50s and '60s. Over those years, I remember seeing a kind of tropical landscape art displayed in banks, motel lobbies and other public spaces. It was just part of the visual cues influencing my everyday life. My normal. The ocean, palms, and seagulls presented a stereotypical view of home environment. Little did anyone know at the time the road the 26 artists responsible for this work would travel. From the late 1950s to the present day, many of them are still painting and traveling. Among them is R. L. Lewis, Jr.

The term "Highwaymen Art" had just become a buzz word during the 1990s. As a part-time artist since the '70s and a full time school administrator, I wanted to learn more about their art and unusual history. I met R. L. Lewis in 2004, in Ocala, at an art exhibition featuring the Highwaymen. Several of the other artists were there, including the sole woman, Mary Ann Carroll. But I was attracted to the more diverse dimension of richness I saw in the work of R. L. Lewis, Jr. In our conversation, I found we had teaching as a common thread. He taught art in Brevard County Schools for many years. Before I knew it, I had scheduled him to "teach" at the local performing arts elementary school where I was principal. He demonstrated his painting skills and techniques for the fourth and fifth grade students on the day he spent with us. I was entranced! I knew I had to learn more from him. Thus began a wonderful friendship. He became my art teacher and mentor.

This publication is an opportunity to enjoy and get to know more about R. L. Lewis, Jr., and his art. His paintings embody a depth and insightful understanding of the Florida where he grew up. The reader can sense being with him among the moss draped oaks and cypress, palms and pines. His paintings take you back to the pristine old Florida of times that are vanishing. These are scenes R. L. and I took for granted when we were growing up. The dramatic colors of the sky are on the edge of extreme, while egrets and herons peacefully enjoy their routines. The subjects of his paintings range from orange groves to remote lakes and swamps, to seashores and beaches, and to historic buildings. The light of R. L. Lewis shines brighter as the years tick by. He is driven to paint, producing hundreds of paintings annually. Even on an occasion when he was hospitalized, he insisted on having color pencils with him, so he could create.

Getting R. L. and his paintings to the public is truly a family affair. His son, Robert Lewis III, is his manager, publicist, promoter, and transporter. Events, art shows, and demonstrations have been on the schedule almost weekly for the past several years. The popularity of the Highwaymen artists keep him and the family very busy. His wife, Ann, almost always accompanies R. L. and is a permanent part of the entourage. Ann has a saintly quiet dignity that contributes to the significance of each event.

The personality of the R. L. Lewis I have gotten to know is one of a very humble, generous man with an easy smile and immense sense of humor. He engages in conversations with people as if he has all day to laugh and tell stories. He is a perpetual teacher willing to share his now famous style of painting. This book is a gift for us all. Let's enjoy the glimpse into the light of this man's world and his work. Shine on R. L., shine on!!

Lynn Herrick, Ed.D
Artist and Educator

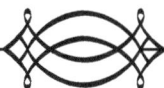

R.L. LEWIS, JR

His Story - His Legacy

R L Lewis Jr. was born February 3, 1941, the third of six children born to Robert L. Lewis Sr., a Florida East Coast Railroad laborer and Marion Lewis, a seamstress. During his primary years, he was raised in City Point, FL. (just north of Cocoa) at Carlton Terrace on Indian River Road. As a little boy, he and his siblings walked a few miles to the City Point historically black one- room Dame School. Robert's family lived on property owned by a white family called the Sherrods. They were allowed to live on the backside of the property, so long as they kept the property clean and in order. Their riverfront home with its tin roof shack consisted of three bedrooms, a wooden stove (used for cooking and heating), an outdoor priming pump for running water, and an outhouse toilet. By the time that R.L. had reached grade school, they had acquired a bathroom with the necessary plumbing.

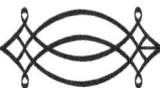

"My mother helped to reinforce my artistic side by

encouraging me to make the toy cars that I wanted.

I would take one block of wood along with jar caps,

a nail and string (used to pull my toy)."

CHAPTER 1

THE WONDER YEARS...IN MY OWN WORDS

Initially as a young boy, I spent lots of time with my older brother, James (by two years), and my younger brother, Morris (by one year), playing in and around the Indian River Lagoon system. A large part of my imagination was influenced because of how I spent all of my time at the lagoon. I distinctly remember the smell of the salt air wafting from the Indian River with the oncoming presence of the summer storms. I remember the salt air comingling with the ripe scent from the mango trees and the beautiful presence of the Royal Poinciana trees. We would run around carefree. We could hear our neighbors' shutters clanging from the challenge of the winds. During these impending storms or blustery days, we would create our own fun game by taking fallen palmetto fronds and sliding down steep spots on the river. Had he known of our adventures, my father would have spanked us. River Road was very dense with lush vegetation, and the river was full of aquatic life—most of which we ate. We sometimes played and went on adventures with two white boys whose last name was Beckman. We would often wade into the lagoon waters retrieving stray boats. We would paddle out towards islands in perilously leaky boats—using our hands or small buckets to stem the tide of these leaks. Once on these islands, we would run around playing before stopping to dig for clay around the island embankments. I would take the clay home on most occasions and sit in the front yard to make my own toys. We didn't have the financial means to purchase toys, so I would attempt to make the toy that I desired. I molded figures of weight lifters and toy soldiers. My mother helped to reinforce my artistic side by encouraging me to make the toy cars that I wanted. I would take one block of wood along with jar caps, a nail and string (used to pull my toy). My mother also encouraged me to draw shapes and figures that I witnessed in my surroundings.

MY ADOLESCENT YEARS

B y the time that I was 13 years old, my father had saved up enough money to purchase approximately ten acres in City Point (about two miles away), in a densely wooded area—away from the Indian River. My brothers and I would occasionally make the trek back to the river, as it had always been a source of environmental comfort and a great food source. A few years after our move to City Point, I began to attend historically-black Monroe High School in Cocoa. In our segregated society, Monroe was one of the three historically-black schools in Brevard County. The other two high schools for blacks were Stone in Melbourne and Gibson in Titusville.

I was a quiet person who was not a very good student. I didn't particularly have a favorite or best subject. I knew that my father preached and demanded that his kids go to school, as he didn't make it past the third grade. He was determined that we would do better than he had. Delinquency was not an option, as he believed in discipline. He had a switch that, as he put it, would, "Learn you some sense!"

CHAPTER 3

MEETING MS. ALBERTA LEISURE

During my junior year (1957-58) at Monroe, I was determined to play football. My older brother, James, was on the team. I thought the uniforms looked pretty good, and besides the team traveled to various towns to play teams all over Central Florida. I was pint sized—not weighing more than 125 pounds "soaking wet!" Nevertheless, I showed up at the weigh-in for all players, hoping that I wouldn't be turned away. Fortunately, Coach Sims was focused on something that was on his clip board. I remember him saying: "Little Lewis, step up... how much do you weigh?" I manipulated the scale and barked out, "140 pounds, Sir!" He slowly glanced up and smirked, "Boy, you couldn't weigh 140 even if you were dipped in thick molasses!" I was expecting to be turned away, but he suddenly said to me, "Fall in!" I got into most games, playing on the defense. By mid-season, I had gotten increased playing time. That all came to an abrupt halt in a game against Inverness, when I was clipped from behind by an offensive player. This caused me to have a high ankle sprain. During those days, you couldn't sit out of football practice idle, as sports was part of the elective credit. I was sent to art class as a result of my injury. Having had to make my own toys during my formative years, I had been creative, so I felt comfortable in art. The teacher for this class was a little (brunette), white lady—named Alberta Leisure. She taught part-time among the three historically-black schools in the county. Most of the class, like me, tended to drift—doing just enough to hopefully get by. On the particular day during the Fall of 1957, she began to illustrate "how to draw an Indian River Lagoon scene with pencil."

This instantly resonated with me, as I had played in and around that river system. It represented a major vein of life to me. I gathered the drawing material that she had passed out to us students. I proceeded to listen and follow closely to her instruction. I had noticed the ease in her voice inflection and how she delivered her instruction. I also noticed how many of my peers seemed to drift away, day dreaming. I thought this was quite interesting. Why weren't they seeing what I was seeing? I followed as she first etched the background, then the middle ground, the foreground, and lastly overlapping with some details in the scene. She walked around, examining the artist paper

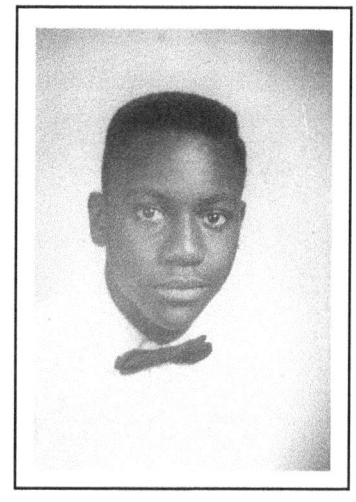

Young RL Lewis

of each student with the eye and interest of a good teacher. She nodded in approval of one or two students, encouraging the many who had only made less than futile attempts. She came to my desk and paused for what seemed like an eternity. I was expecting her to give me one of those subtle words of encouragement like that of so many of the other students, but I got the most enchanting warm smile of approval—a Job Well Done smile. She posted my drawing on the bulletin board. I left class feeling like art class was the place to be, outside of lunch. It felt good getting the teacher's approval! The next art class session, Ms. Leisure brought water color sets to class. She directed the class to a color wheel, including how to mix colors. I felt very engaged and was in tuned to this paint session. She proceeded as she had previously done with the background, firstly, using water to moisten the artist paper, before proceeding to the white paint that set the stage for her use of the blue that mingled her skyline. Her middle ground was highlighted by a term she used called atmospheric perspective. Her foreground had subtle palms surrounded by dense Indian River vegetation— just like I had remembered as a kid. Finally, she overlapped the scene with the Spanish moss we'd used as kids to box with and used as gauze for our scrapes from an occasional accident.

I was so engrossed in following her artistic instruction that I had finished the scene well before any other student. Some of the students peered over to view my work. They were surprised. Ms. Leisure slowly made her way around the classroom in the same manner as she had before. This time she approached my desk with a keen interest. She picked up my work and held it up in amazement. Many of the students oohed and aahed! I had painted my first Florida landscape! I took the painting home for my mother. I told her that I had been able to mimic what I had seen the teacher paint in class. She gave me the most approving smile and hug. I had always shown my homemade toys and various drawings and later paintings to my mother. She was inspirational. I have always said that Ms. Leisure was that "push/pull" effect that I had to have in my life in order to expose my artistic gift. She proceeded to encourage me to draw and paint sights and scenes in the community. One of the most significant paintings in high school was my high school principal, Mr. B.A. Moss. I presented a 8 x 10 watercolor portrait to him in 1958. He thought this was pretty neat and thoughtful of me. A lady in the community named Ms. Thompson, got wind of my artistic skills. I had just painted (in 1958) the "Last Supper." She offered me two dollars for this painting. I thought I should've gotten more, but I gladly accepted the money.

CHAPTER 4

WORKING TO MAKE ENDS MEET

During my high school days, I felt that I needed to work to make ends meet. During my junior year (1957-1958), I acquired a handyman job with an affluent gentleman named C. B. Litz. He paid me five dollars per week, every Saturday morning. He would also pay me an additional two dollars for every evening that I would eat supper with him. He was a man who possessed a very temperate spirit. He saw me as a young man who had potential. He told me that I could do anything I focused my attention on and worked hard for. Additionally, every weekend I worked at Hubs Inn Restaurant (1910-1968). It was located on the Indian River Lagoon in Cocoa. It was known as the destination point in Brevard County for delicious seafood. In my artistic life, it has become a part of some of my favorite scenes to paint.

The Ben Issac Effect

During my senior year, Ms. Leisure approached me with the idea of attending an art school in Kentucky. I was interested, but I had great reservations, as my father only made $40.00 per week working for Florida East Coast Railroad. My mother was a seamstress. They did the best that they could for us. I shied away from this idea and was resigned to the idea of considering some type of service-related job in Cocoa. At the end of my senior year, my best friend Eugene Grant's uncle,

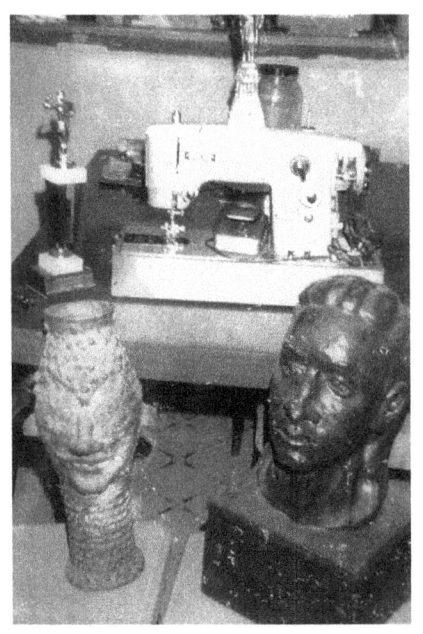

RL Lewis sculpting figures during his college days.

Ben Isaac, approached us with the idea of at least considering college. He noted that we had to at least give it (college) a shot before we settled for a job in the community. Mr. Isaac helped Eugene and me fill out the necessary paperwork to attend historically black Edward Waters College in Jacksonville. My father put together a "care package" that consisted of saltines, sardines, peanut butter, grape jelly, and potted meat, along with five dollars. He was very proud of me attending college. He patted me on the back and told me to, "Go make it work!" I had no clue of what I should major in, so I took General Studies/Core Pre-requisite.

CHAPTER

SCHOOL DAZE

I attended Edward Waters for one year and an additional semester (1959-1960) before I ran out of financial resources. During my tenure at this institution, I met a fellow student by the name of Charlie Wells. I later met his brother, fellow Highwaymen artist S. M. Wells, with whom I painted with for more than 20 years.

Northern Migration

Some of my college friends and I decided that we would migrate up north for job opportunities in 1961. One of the guys had relatives in New Jersey, so we decided we would go there. We got jobs at the same restaurant and resided in Wildwood, New Jersey, for six months. After things thinned out in Wildwood, we wound up traveling to Syracuse, NY. I did not want to return to Florida. I contacted Mr. Ben Issac (Eugene's uncle) as he was working at an upstate memorial hospital in Syracuse. He helped me acquire an upstairs one bedroom flat for eight dollars per month. I quickly got employed. I later wound up working at the Syracuse University Hospital as an orderly. During this time, one of the university administrative supervisors on my floor called me into her office to discuss my application. I sat in her office not knowing why I was summoned to her office. She stated that she noticed that I had some college behind me. She wanted me to know that the University "subsidized" the education of its employees. I had no idea what that meant until she elaborated.

The Syracuse University Experience

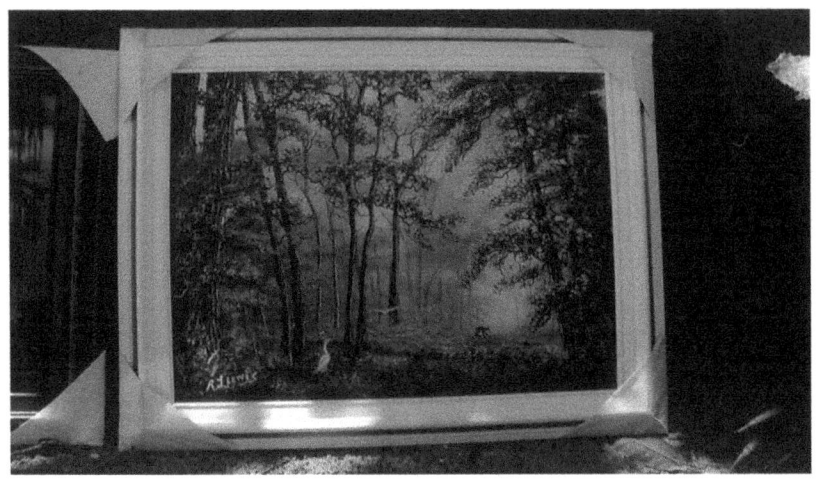

1970 Fawn in the Forrest Mist

I registered for classes in 1962 at Syracuse under this subsidy. I decided to major in Art Education after I had completed my basic core classes. It was what I knew. Art was my therapy. I was still drawing and sketching sites and scenes from my high school days.

During my Northern journey, I simply sketched this new landscape that was before me. I attended Syracuse for three years (mostly part-time) while working. During my tenure at Syracuse, I branched out deeper into my artistic craft. Outside of drawing and sketching, I learned how to sculpt, make jewelry, and even some woodwork. I began to use other painting mediums such as oils and acrylics. I had painted my first Florida landscape (1958) with watercolor. I especially liked oils because of their fluid feel. Learning and eventually mastering oils, watercolors, and acrylics, I became a more proficient artist.

Finishing up at FAMU

By 1965, I wanted to return to Florida and knew that I was at least a year worth of credits short of my bachelors of art degree in Art Education. I decided to attend historically black Florida A&M University

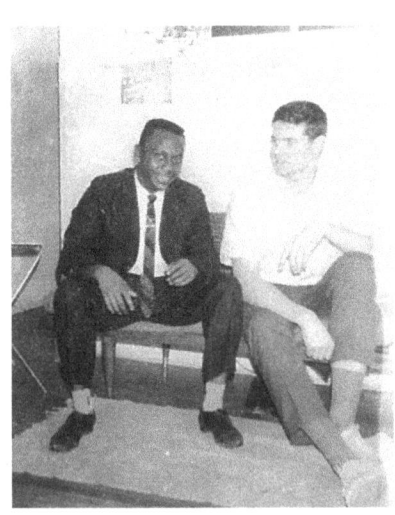

RL and a fellow student at Syracuse University.

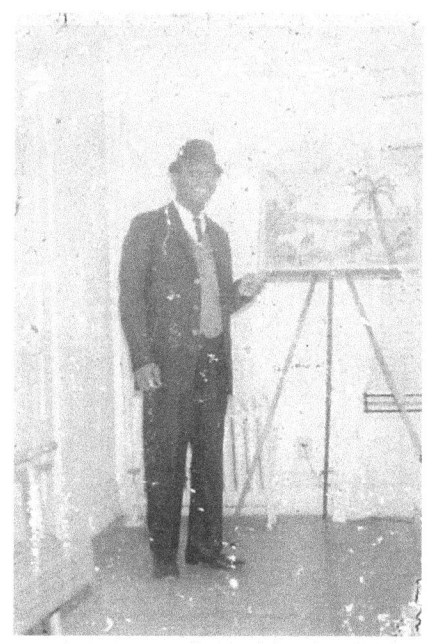

RL at FAMU

in Tallahassee, Florida. During my last year of college, I began to study some of the great artists in world history, such as Rembrandt and Picasso. I began to pay close attention to the composition and balance in my sketches and paintings. I started to focus on the balance between light and dark in the various landscapes that I painted during that time. I graduated from Florida A&M University with a Bachelor's of Arts Degree in 1966.

Returning home to the "Space Coast"

I moved back to Brevard County, Cocoa, Florida. Because of the Kennedy Space Center, Brevard County was now being called the Space Coast. During the next couple of years, I worked for Pan Am, Bendix Corporation, and finally Boeing. At Boeing, I was a graphic illustrator—working with graft charts, graft bars, drafting tables, and T-squares. After more than a year, Boeing asked me to consider a transfer to Seattle, Washington, as they told me I had a greater chance of being placed on a fast track for promotions. During this time, I began to inquire and ultimately acquire a position in the Brevard County school system as a teacher. I began teaching full time in the school system during the 1968-1969 school year. I had also been dabbling with painting Florida landscapes since my return to Brevard County. I started to sell these paintings to individuals who liked these paintings.

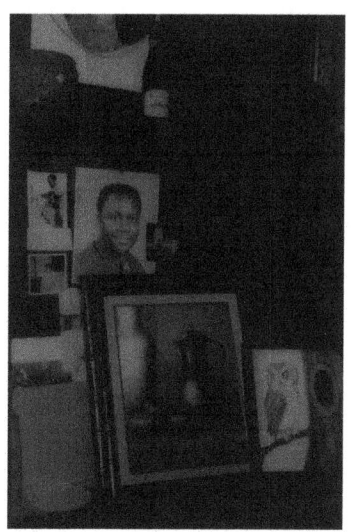

RL Lewis still life painting in the late 1960's.

TEAMING UP WITH S.M. WELLS

I had also met S. M. Wells upon my return to the area. He was a sign painter at the time. He and I would occasionally get together and try our lot at painting landscapes. In 1968, he came to visit me and said that he had seen a couple of artists named the Newton brothers, painting at a housing complex called "Little Vietnam." It had acquired this name for its penchant for violence. Nevertheless, I went to see if I could witness these guys in action. Upon my arrival, I noticed that they had a wooden palate with Upson board tacked on. I paid close attention to their technique. Harold Newton was painting alongside his brother, Sam. I paid particular attention to Harold's technique. I had heard of his legend ten years before from Ms. Leisure giving me a newspaper clipping of him. This was a Miami Herald newspaper clipping that

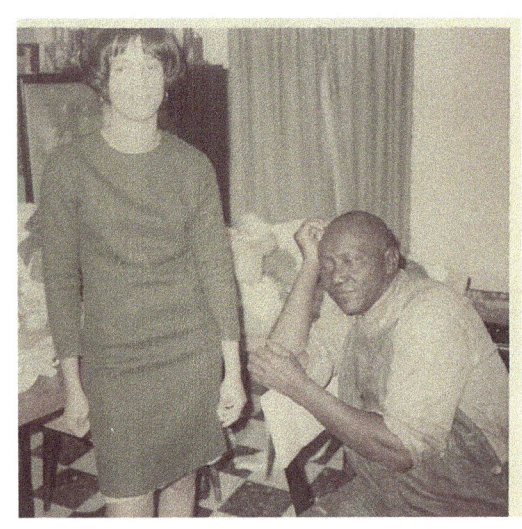

My wife Ann with my father Robert Sr.

said, "Artist Pays Doctor Bills with His Artwork." This was very inspirational to me, as I got to see a black man doing what I didn't think was possible. Needless to say, I mustered up a conversation with them. They eventually gave me a brush to see what I could do! I wound up painting my first Florida landscape with oils on Upson board with H. Newton's brush. I went back to show Wells this painting. This encounter helped me to improve my painting technique. I began to look more closely into painting as an enterprise. I began to team with S. M. Wells on the weekends. We would paint with the idea of selling these paintings. We began to sell our paintings to banks, attorneys, and businesses in Brevard County and other surrounding counties such as, Volusia (Daytona Beach), Orange (Orlando), and Duval (Jacksonville).

An Honest Hustle

We called our selling of our artwork an "honest hustle," simply because we were using almighty God's gift of painting to make a living while pleasing the client. Painting landscapes became Wells's full-time profession. I did not quit my full-time job as a junior high school art teacher. I simply painted Florida landscapes in the back of the classroom, where I had created a platform to paint scenes. During the school week, I painted randomly with the idea of selling to a prospective client after school or on the weekend. I did most of my selling during school breaks and most especially the summer break, where I could go full tilt. During the school year, I ordered stretch canvas. I was able to place these orders as a part of my lesson planning. I spent time, at least a couple of weeks, teaching the wet on wet technique to my students, so canvas was required during this time. I would occasionally paint on Upson board, but by the mid-1970s, I began to paint exclusively on either canvas board or stretch canvas. S.M. and I developed a paint/selling motto of "paint it fast, sell it cheap!" In the mid to late 1960s, I began to notice the works of other Florida landscape artists in many of the banks where we ventured to sell our artwork. I began to paint smaller sizes (i.e. 5 x 7's and 8 x 10's.) I thought this was a way of politely getting into the pockets of clients that already had a larger piece of artwork on their business walls. The 5 x 7's sold for

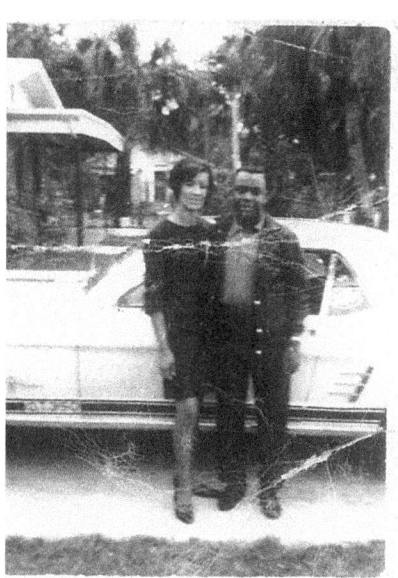

My wife and I standing in front of my 65 Mustang.

27

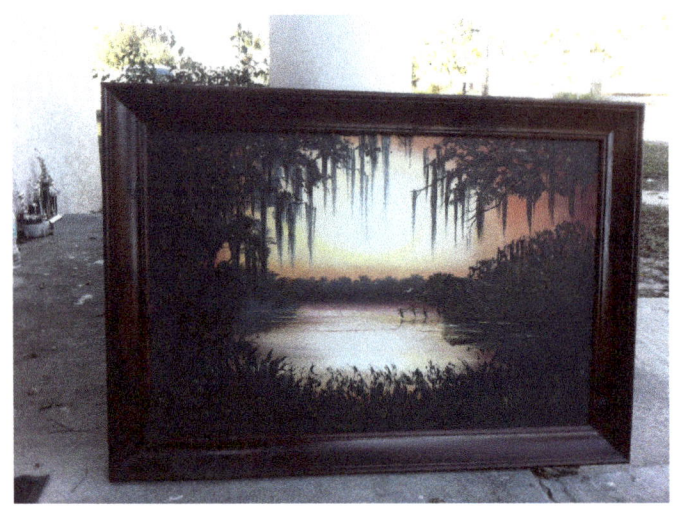

1975 St. Johns River on Canvas Panel

five dollars, while the 8 x 10's sold one for ten dollars or two for sixteen dollars. Other standard sizes were: 12 x 24, 16 x 20, 18 x 24, 24 x 30, 24 x 36 and 24 x 48. During the late '60s and early '70s, prices ranged from ten to fifteen dollars for a 12 x 24 to as much as seventy-five dollars for a 24 x 48. *The Paint Shack* on my property was the place where we primarily used to paint these various sized paintings. We erected a series of 1 x 2 foot wood strips around the walls. These was used to tack Upson board, canvas panels, and Masonite. We also created shelves that protruded from the walls, used to house our painting palates. We generally started painting the smaller sizes (quick sellers) first and ultimately graduated to larger sizes during our paint sessions. This was largely based on supply and demand. On a Friday evening or Saturday morning, we could paint as many as 50 to 60 paintings between us! We acquired many of our frames from a white gentleman named Jim Leverage. He owned a frame shop across from the Greyhound bus station in Cocoa.

CHAPTER 7

TRANSFERRING TO ROOSEVELT

After two years of teaching at Kennedy Junior High School, I transferred to Roosevelt Junior High School in Cocoa Beach, Florida. I was one of two black instructors in the school. The school's population was approximately 95 percent white. Nevertheless, I wound up teaching at this institution for 22 years. I worked alongside some of the best educators and students during my 32 year tenure as an educator. My client base as a Florida landscape painter began to change, as the beachside communities were very receptive to purchasing my artwork. I painted everything from a Banana River mangrove scene, to Charley the Blue Heron, to the mascot for Cocoa Beach High School. I had always considered myself a versatile artist, because of my ability to paint portraits, landscapes, still life, and monuments in the community. This was reaffirmed even more, as one of my beachside clients commissioned me to paint the checkerboard designed Cocoa Beach pier at sunrise. The more I painted Commissioned requests, the more I began to play a game of "begots." Simply explained, it's when a client is pleased with your work, you politely ask that they tell their friends about you. Thus, one client ultimately begot another. S.M. Wells and I also coined a phrase called "floating." We would make random, targeted stops in business complexes or districts where we believed there was a prospective client base that would be receptive to purchasing our artwork. We did not always encounter friendly faces, but we would simply ask if someone was interested in taking a look at the artwork that we painted. If the business owner was receptive, we would show our pieces.

CHAPTER 8

THE ART OF THE SALE

I was very shy as a kid, but I had developed into an extroverted person by the time that I had graduated from college. As a result, I was not afraid to engage the public—regardless of their race. Of course, I had grown up in the segregated South, and I knew that there were places that I would not be accepted. I also felt that my God-given ability to paint Florida landscapes had a way of making me colorless. The paintings were about the landscapes in Florida that I shared with the white citizenry. I felt that, as long as I kept the focus on the paintings' depiction and not myself, I was going to be successful. In the late 1960s and throughout the 1970s, I felt that my art was aesthetically pleasing to prospective clients. I was a willing listener, and I would readily paint what the client desired. I also felt that my versatility, my ability to paint anything, was an advantage. If I happened upon a client who was "just looking," I would say, "Hypothetically, if you were buying one of the paintings, what would it be?" They would invariably point out the piece that they would like to purchase. I would then make them a deal by giving them an attractive price point.

Robbing Them Without a Gun

Selling paintings in banks was a challenge, yet a fun experience. I used to say that selling paintings in banks was equal to "robbing them without a gun!" If I sold a painting in a certain town or city, I would take the check from the client to their respective bank. I would take at least two or more paintings (back to back) with a spandex band and venture into the bank, irrespective of the No Solicitation sign. If I was stopped and told of the policy of no solicitation, I would simply show the client check and state, "So you don't honor your checks?" Bank personnel would apologize and politely retreat. I would then rest the paintings on the floor next to me, as I was cashing the check. Someone would ask me if I painted them or comment on how beautiful the scenes were. Eventually, I would establish a relationship with the bank higher ups and they would allow me to come in despite the No Solicitation sign. At times, they would tell me what days to come in. I asked one bank administrator why he wanted me to come in on Thursdays, and he smiled and said, "Because that's when everybody gets paid!" Attorneys and accountants offices were also very good places to sell artwork. They were always buying for their offices or as gifts for friends and family. I often played the game of "begots" with them. They would openly send me to someone else in their trade. They would also be the ones to commission me to paint portraits of their kids or the family pet.

CHAPTER 9

MEETING BOB DANCE

One of my most memorable sells was in 1974. I needed a new car. I was watching TV at home on a Saturday, when I saw a car dealership owner named Bob Dance make his commercial sales pitch. I noticed that he performed most of these commercials with his pet named "Buster, the Wonder Dog." The dog was dressed in a super hero cape. I told my wife that I was going to Longwood, Florida, the next Saturday to meet this car dealer. I ventured over to his dealership with the intent to meet him. I was accosted by a few of his salesmen, but I told them that I was interested in meeting him before I would consider

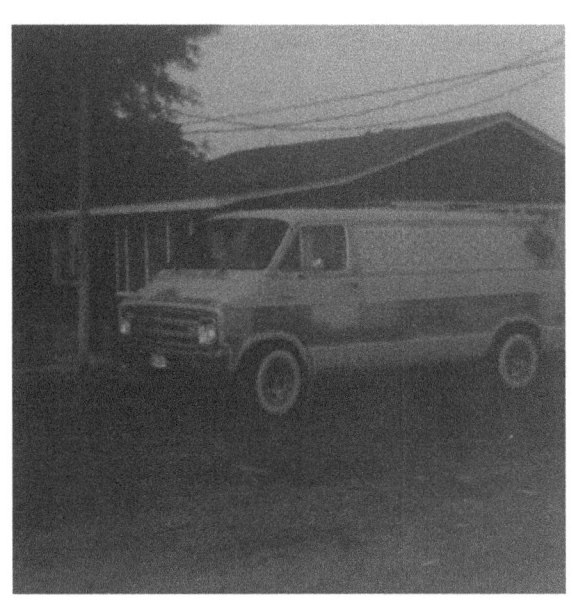

Custom made Dodge van purchased from Bob Dance Dodge.

purchasing a vehicle. I was able to have a sit down conversation with him. I told him that I would like to make him a deal. He was intrigued and said, "What's your proposition?" "I want to paint, Buster, the Wonder Dog for you in all of his glory." He was intrigued and then ecstatic. He was touched; he loved the idea. He told me that if I painted his dog to his specification, he would sell me a vehicle of my choosing on his lot at a dollar over his invoice price. Needless to say, I painted his prized pet to specification and was able to leave the dealership with a custom made van (white wall tires, big stereo system, a fridge and a TV). I was also able to sell some of his salesmen some of my landscapes as well.

CHAPTER 10

TEACHING AT BREVARD COMMUNITY COLLEGE

In the late 1970s, I was blessed with the opportunity to teach the "wet on wet" technique in the adult education program at Brevard Community College (BCC) in Cocoa, Florida. I taught classes twice per week in the evenings. Teaching adults was fun yet challenging. Some of my adult students were quick studies. I often focused on a myriad of sights and scenes each week, but there were

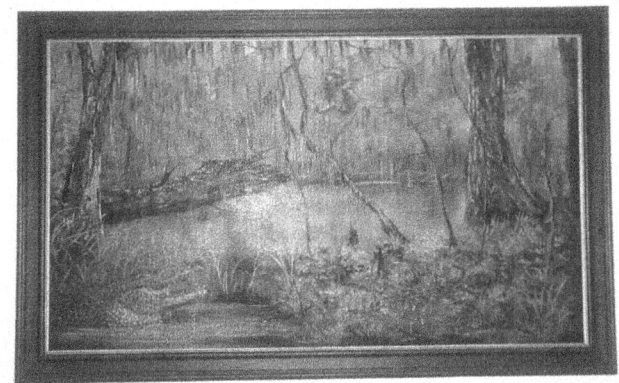

Life Perilous Moments Part 1

times that students had a desire to deviate from the classroom agenda. This forced me to become that much more versatile with my teaching methods. My tenure as a part time instructor lasted from 1978-1991. Many of my adult art students went on to become accomplished artists in their own rights, some even participating in art exhibits and shows around Florida and other parts of the country as well.

Glen Turner

One of my students was a nice gentleman named Glen Turner. He was a very good landscape artist. He spent three years in these evening classes. Each year, he would sit in the front area of the classroom—once directly behind me, and the other two times, at either my right hand or left hand side. He paid very close attention to my technique. I was never concerned with any of my students "stealing my technique." I am very thankful that almighty God loaned me this wonderful gift of painting! Besides, "a gift from God is meant to be shared, not snared!" Nevertheless, my oldest son—Robert L. Lewis III was in a seafood restaurant in the late 1990s when he noticed what he described as a beautiful beach scene. He noted that this painting looked remarkably similar to one of my paintings. He stated that the artists initials on the painting were G.T. I smiled and told him that I was very familiar with this artist, as he was one of my former students. He then responded that there was just one problem with the scene. I asked what he meant by this and he stated that the seagulls left something to be desired. I laughed and said, "Oh yeah, I didn't show him everything!" We still chuckle about this from time to time. Interestingly enough, many of my students helped me to garner clients who would commission me to paint Florida landscapes or some other type of painting. After teaching adults at BCC, I later taught from 1991-2000 at the Adult Art Association in downtown Cocoa Village.

Tools of the trade

In the late 1960s and early 1970s, I would go to East Coast Lumber Company where I would purchase for nine cents a foot of crown molding and seven cents a foot for bed molding. Creating my own frames was a way to manage my cost in some ways. This was an entrepreneurial venture. My objective was to make money with the lowest expenditures. I also purchased brad nails for attaching the frames. I also had a miter box with slotted angles on it. Most of the time, I used the 45 degree angle. I also purchased Upson board by the sheet. I would also venture into J.M. Fields to purchase canvas panels, assorted paint thinner, linseed oil, and multiple tubes of paint.

The Paint Shack and the Classrooms

The junior high and the college classrooms were some of the best places to paint. They offered proper lighting, water, desks, and easels. All of these resources are necessary for good painting. As I mentioned earlier, I also had a *Paint Shack* on my property. It was formerly an unfinished rental that S.M. and I adapted to fit our artistic painting agenda.

CHAPTER 11

HIGHWAYMEN/THE RENAISSANCE PERIOD

My son, Robert L. Lewis III, began teaching high school at Lincoln Park Academy in Fort Pierce, Florida. (1995). During this time, he would eat breakfast at a restaurant up the block from the school called the House of Foods. The restaurant owner's name was (Highwaymen) Hezekiah Baker. My son established a friendly relationship with Mr. Baker. One day during the middle of the school year, Robert III stopped by the restaurant for a bite to eat. He noticed that Mr. Baker had

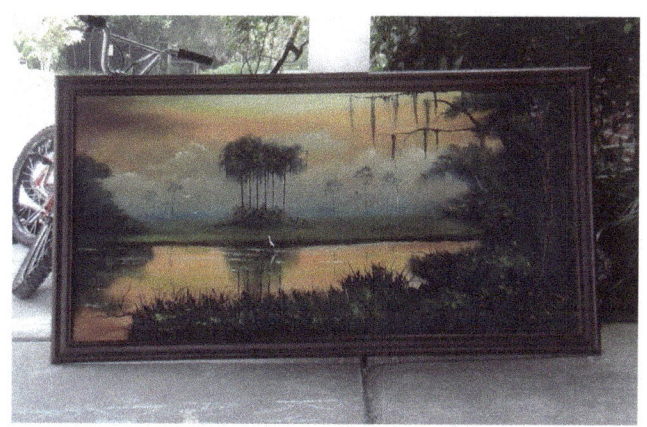

1973 RL Lewis Backwoods painting

some Florida landscape paintings shown on his restaurant walls. My son inquired with interest about these paintings. He asked Hezekiah, "What do you call your paintings?" Hezekiah replied that they were called Highwaymen paintings! My son told him that he knew of a couple of artists on the Space Coast that were painting landscapes very similar to his paintings. Hezekiah responded that he was going to introduce Robert III to many artists in Fort Pierce doing work just like his. I was very intrigued to hear about Hezekiah and other artists in

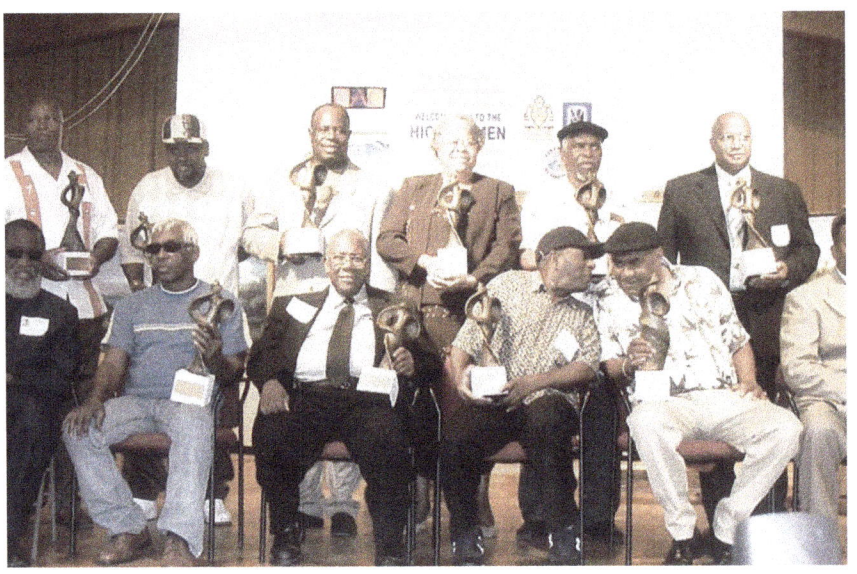

Photo session with many of the original Highwaymen artists in 2007

Fort Pierce, as I had not ever met these artists. I had only known of S.M. Wells and the marvelous works of the three Newton brothers that had moved to Brevard County in the 1960s. I was intrigued by the works of some of the other artists in banks and other places that I had traveled.

In the spring of 1995, Robert III came by my *Paint Shack* to retrieve some of my paintings. This was not unusual, as he would sell a painting here and there for me if he saw where there was an opportunity. He told me that one of his teaching peers had seen some of my paintings in his classroom and wanted him to stop by her house to show more pieces. The next weekend, he came back to Cocoa to visit, noting that he was unsuccessful in selling any of my works. He noted that she had shown him some spectacular works of an artist named, A. E. Backus. My response to my son was, "Is he as good as Harold Newton?" He smiled and told me Backus was very much on par.

During the latter part of the 1990s, I noticed that I could get more money for my paintings. Individuals were calling and asking to stop by the house to purchase a painting. By 1999, I could sell a 36 x 24 for as much as $300 to $400 dollars. Some ten years earlier, I was getting $75.

Daytona State College Professor, Gary Monroe, began visiting me during 1999-2000. The nickname Highwaymen was being heard by me and others ever more. In 2001, I attended Holy Trinity Episcopal School for a book signing with Hezekiah Baker and Mary Ann Carroll for the Highwaymen book by Gary Monroe. I quickly realized that the term Highwaymen and subsequent book by Mr. Monroe had propelled my art and that of my peers into a Renaissance mode! Core groups of collectors helped to propel Highwaymen art to the mainstream. On March 24, 2004, the Highwaymen artists were all inducted into the Florida Artists Hall of Fame!

During this Renaissance period, I have developed a theme. It is "to capture Florida as art history on canvas before it disappears!" This has resonated with many organizations. I have worked successfully with preservation/restoration organizations such as the citrus industry, Florida Cattleman's Association, and several state affiliated organizations. I have also worked with art leagues and art associations around the state. I receive lots of commission requests via the electronic/computer age. They are generally emails that say: "Dear Mr. Lewis, I live, work, or play in the middle of a picture—can you paint it?" If we can agree on the size of the painting and price, I honor their commission request.

CHAPTER 12

WHAT I THINK ABOUT MY GIFT

Every time I paint, I see Almighty God's hands on each of my works. I can't help but think just how great God is because He loaned me this wonderful, creative gift as an artist. This gift has been a great provider for my family and me. It also has positively affected the lives of those who have purchased these anointed paintings. I appreciate everyone who has shared my history with his or her patronage and willingness to feature my artwork in a positive light. I live by one rule only. "There is nothing that is ever too big or too bold, that when it is dedicated to almighty God, it shall be great!"

R.L. LEWIS PRESENTS

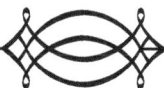

The following plates, are but a fraction of the

thousands of paintings that R.L. Lewis has created.

Almighty God has touched his heart, mind and

hands, as he paints orange groves,

rivers, backwoods and beaches.

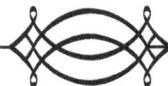

RL denotes that true Floridians

recognize our state's natural beauty

resides in our wild interior.

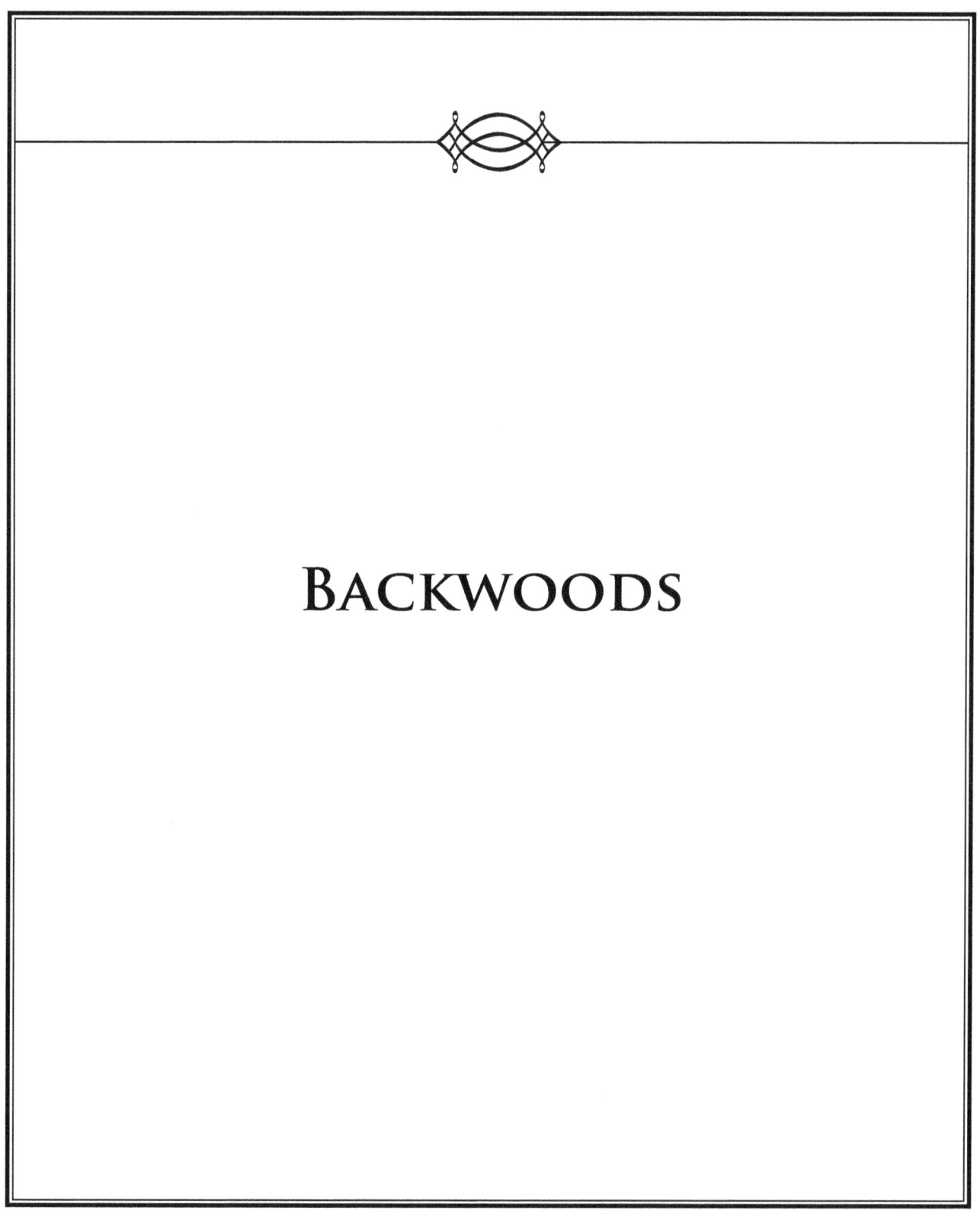

BACKWOODS

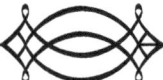

CRACKER SHACK
NEAR THE AUCILLA RIVER

Acrylic on Canvas, 20" x 16"

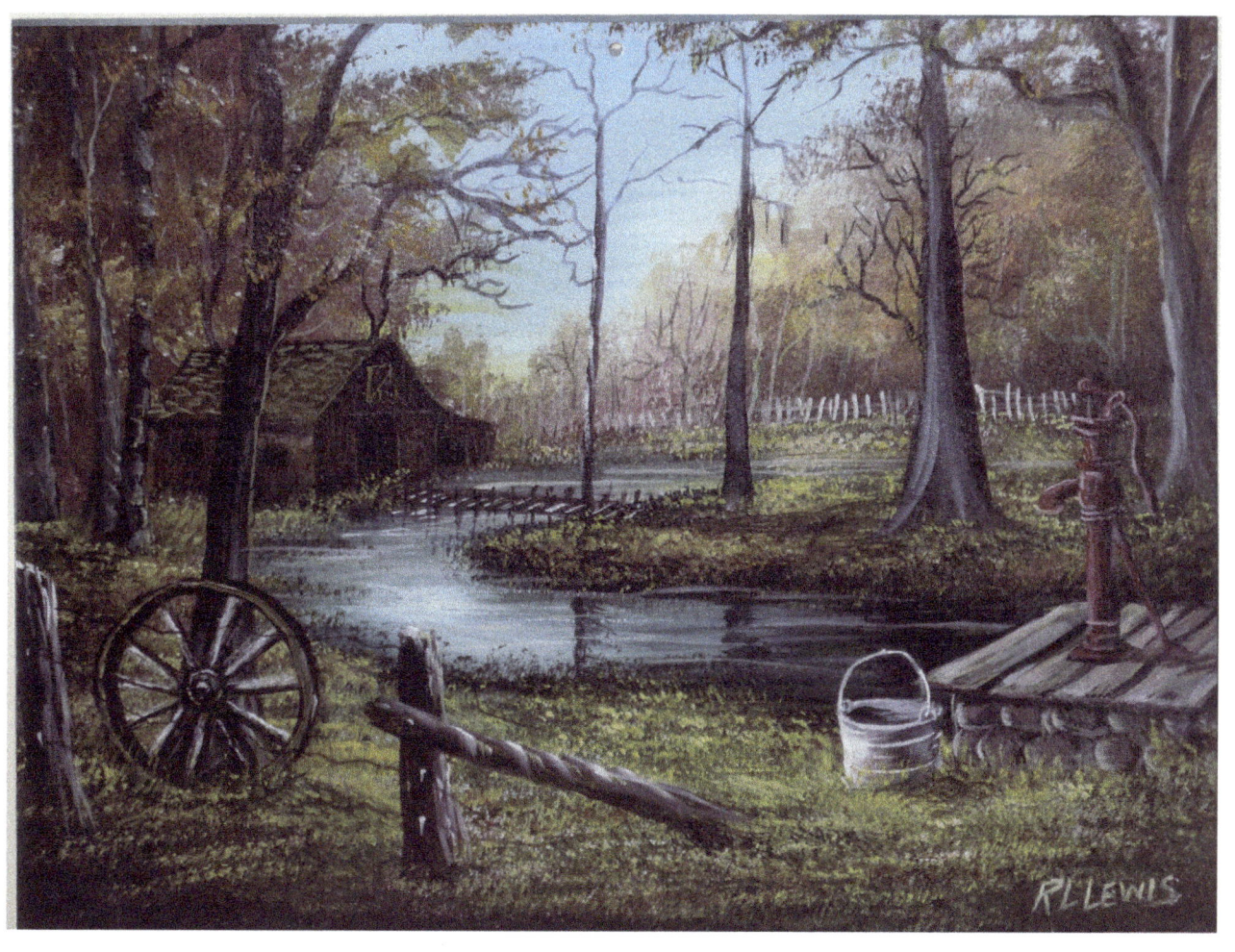

DID YOU KNOW:

*RL enjoys painting fall North Florida landscapes.
He notes that, "The terrain is decidedly different from
Central and South Florida."*

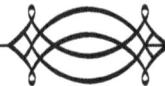

Brahma On The Nature Coast
Hernando County Wetlands

Mixed Media, 40" x 30"

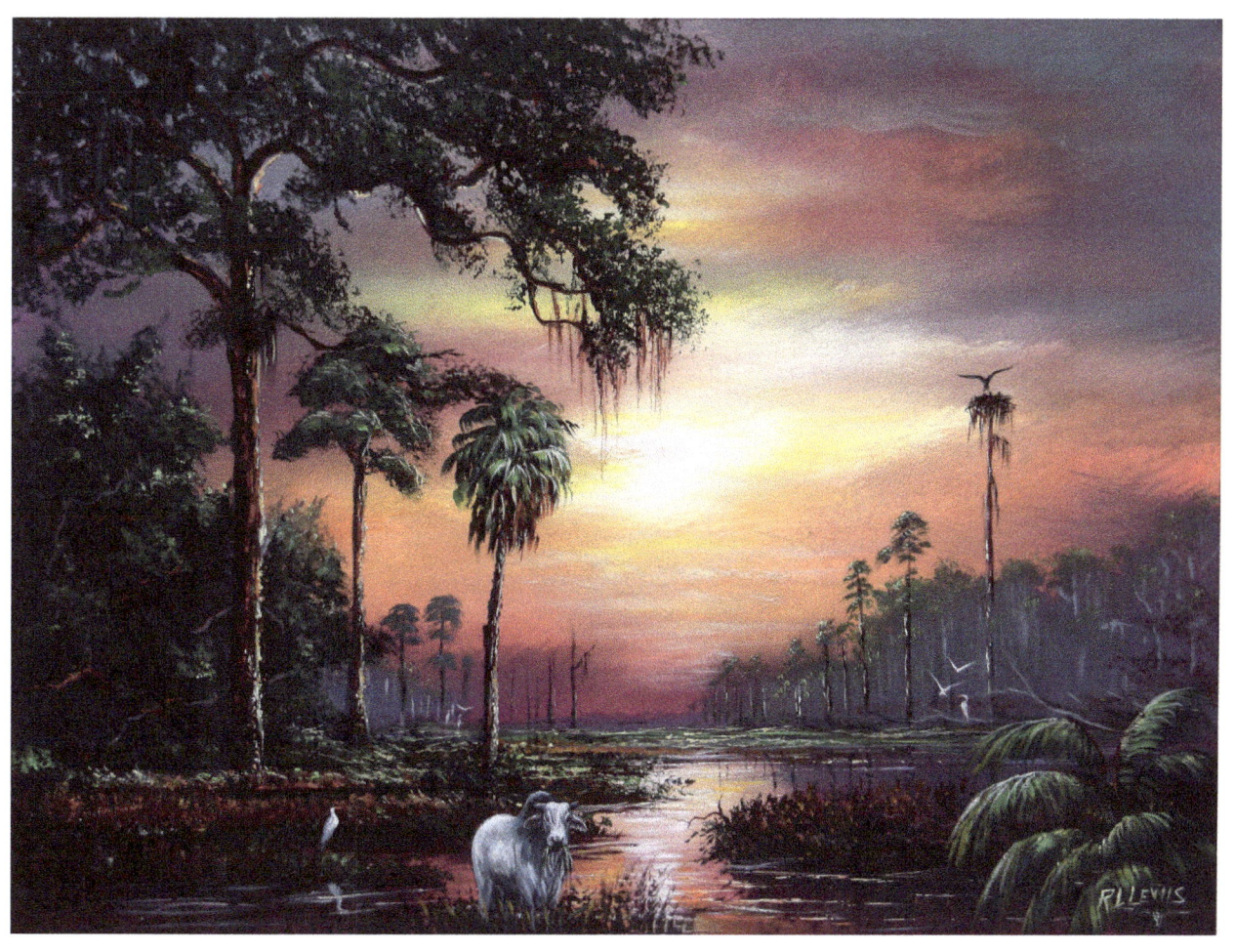

DID YOU KNOW:

RL Lewis is one of the few original Highwaymen artist who specializes in painting domestic and wildlife scenes.

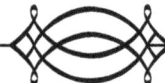

Florida Cowboys Retrieving The Strays Okeechobee Cow Pasture

Oil on Stretch Canvas, 24" x 18"

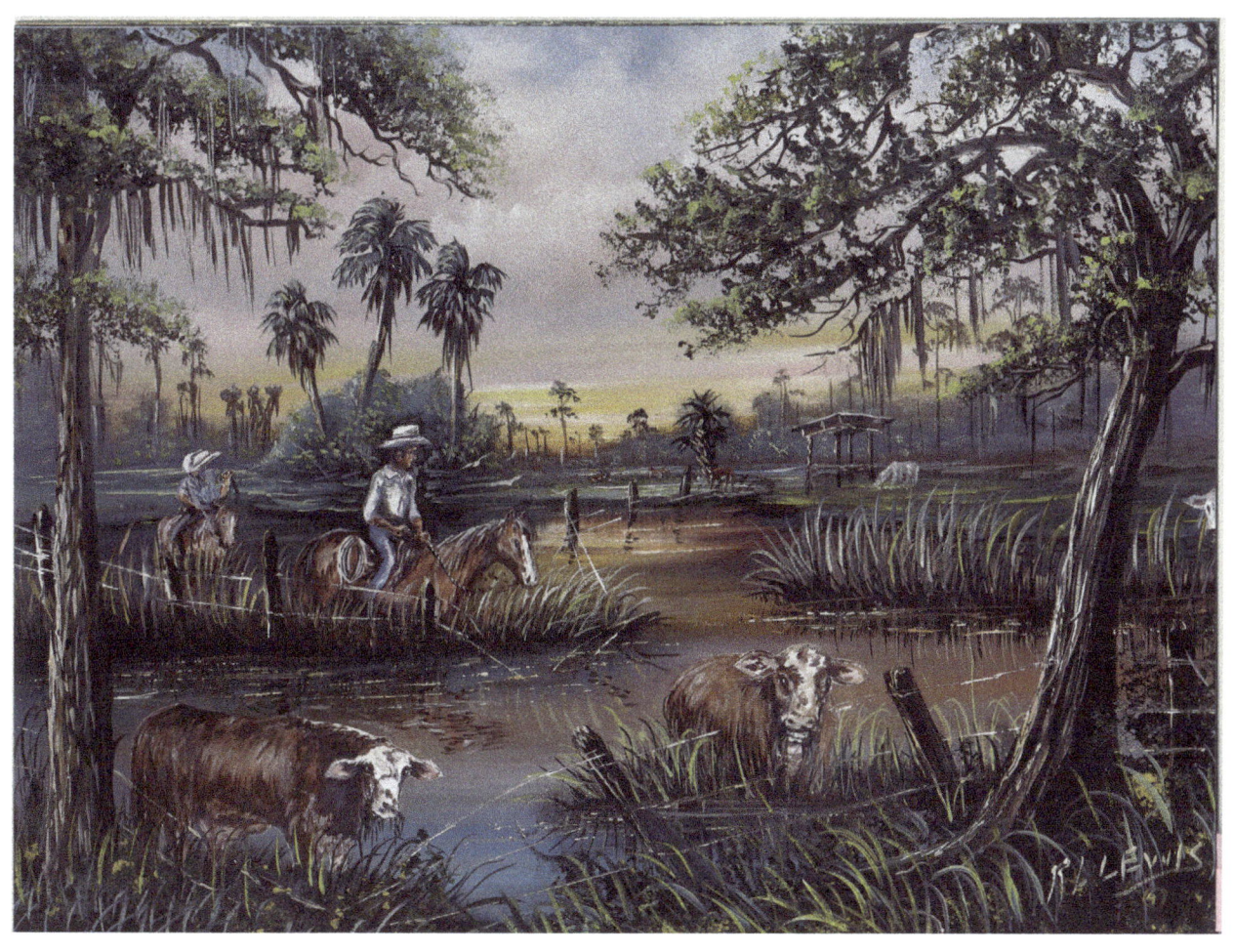

Did You Know:

RL Lewis is well known for his realistic depictions of "Cracker Cowboy" paintings!

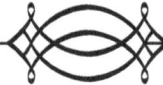

FLORIDA EVERGLADES SUNSET

8 Foot 1965 Original Crocodile Skin
Mixed Media

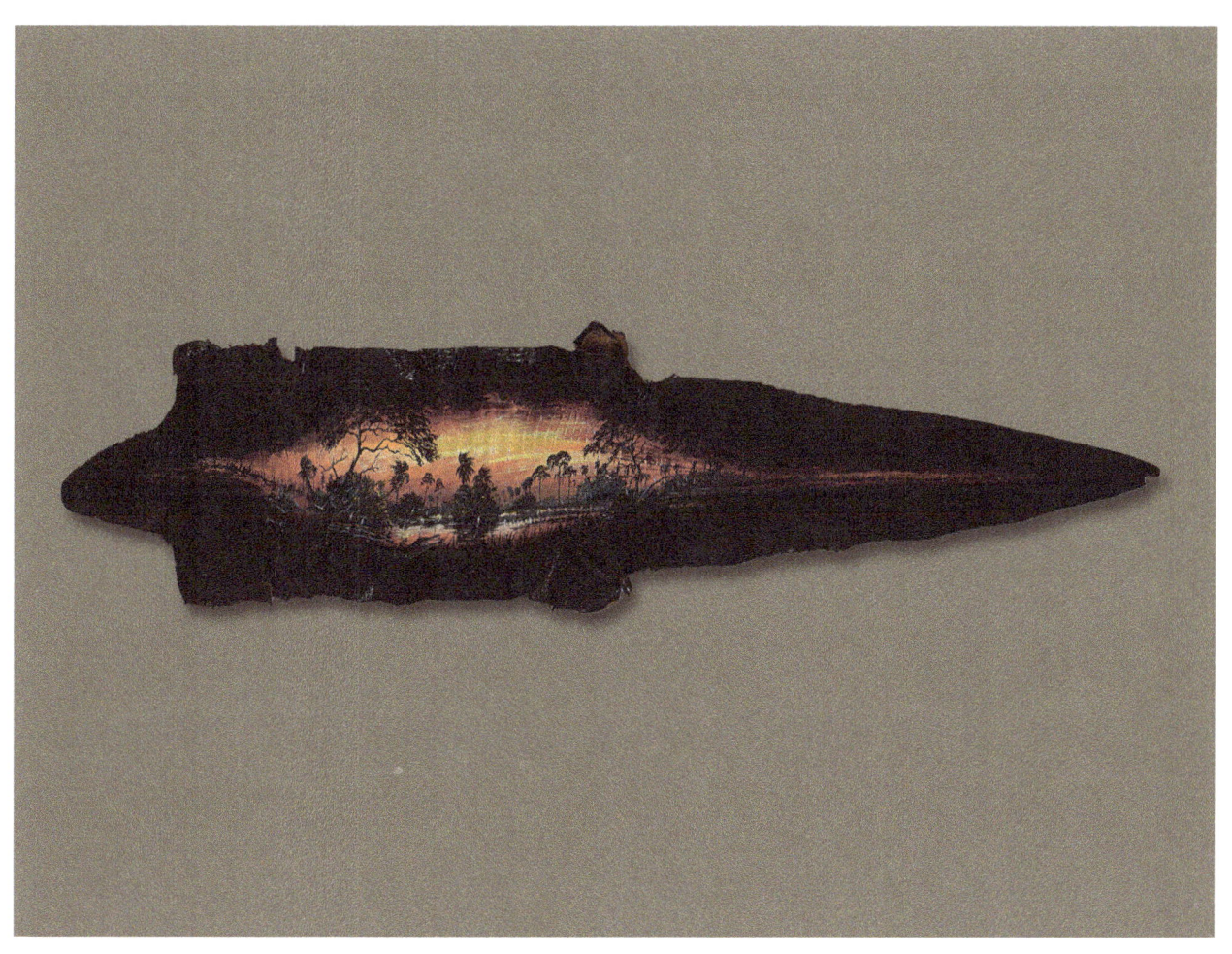

DID YOU KNOW:

This painting represents one of the more eccentric paintings that RL has painted in his career. He has been known to paint on knap sacks, upson board, masonite and artist paper as well.

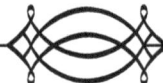

HEREFORD BULL—SIRE OF THE PASTURE ON THE NATURE COAST DADE CITY, FL

Oil on Canvas, 38" x 26"
Mixed Media

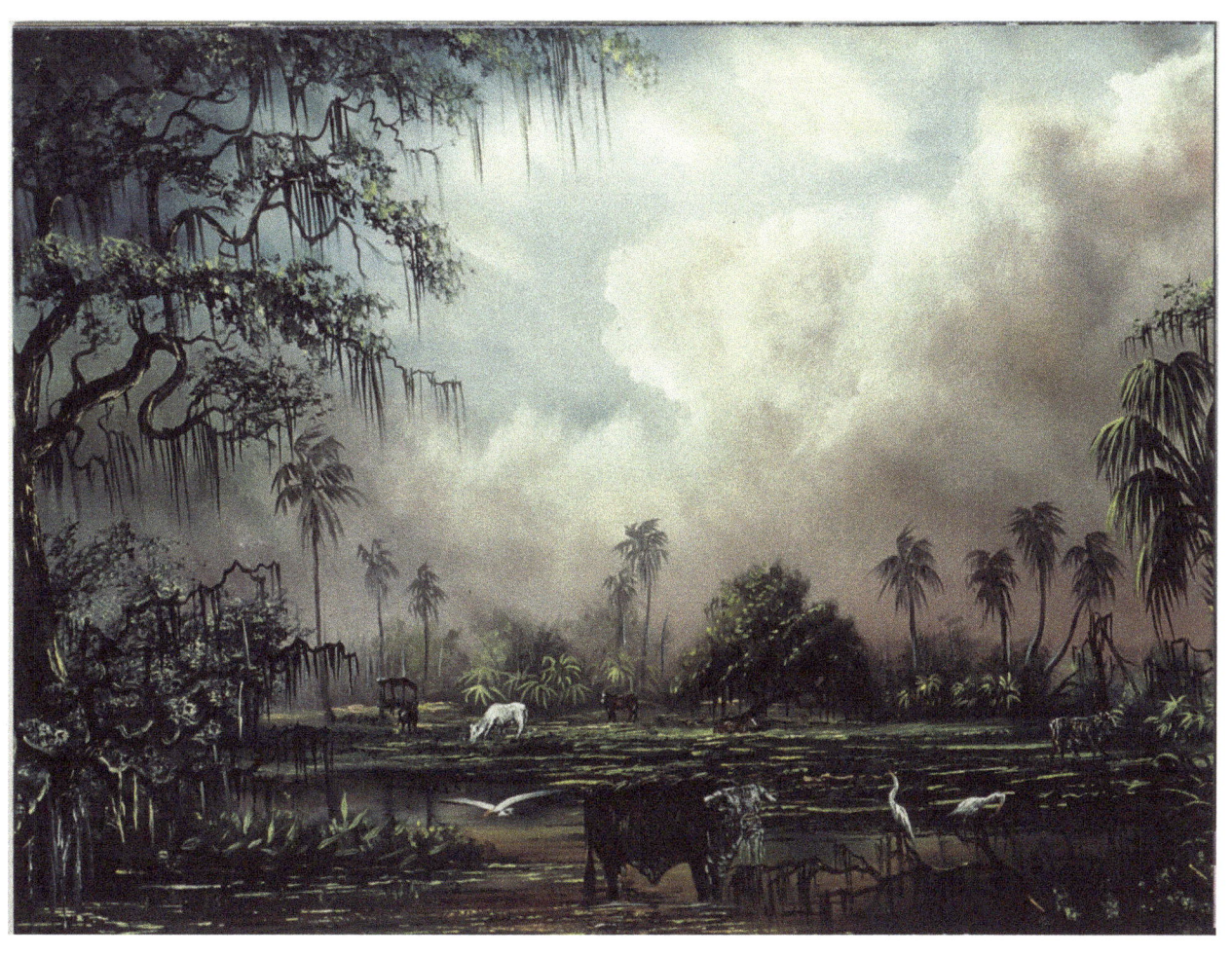

DID YOU KNOW:

In his earlier days of painting, RL would occasionally paint plein aire.

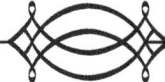

Ocala Cowboys Tending The Pasture

Acrylic on Canvas, 37.75" x 26.75"

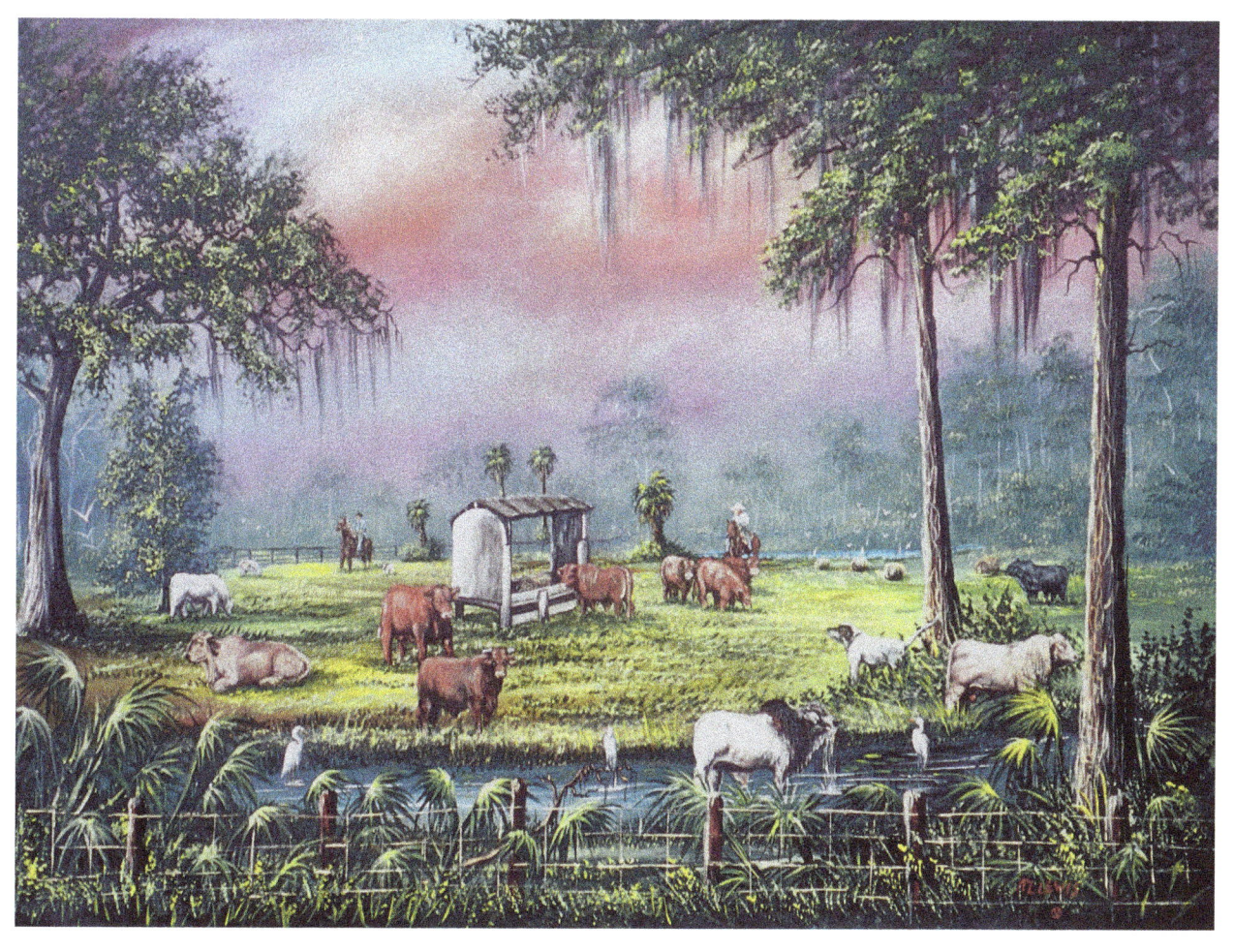

DID YOU KNOW:

This painting is representative of the types of cows that may exist in a cow pasture.

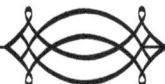

PAYNES PRARIE STATE PRESERVE

Acrylic on Canvas, 20" x 16"

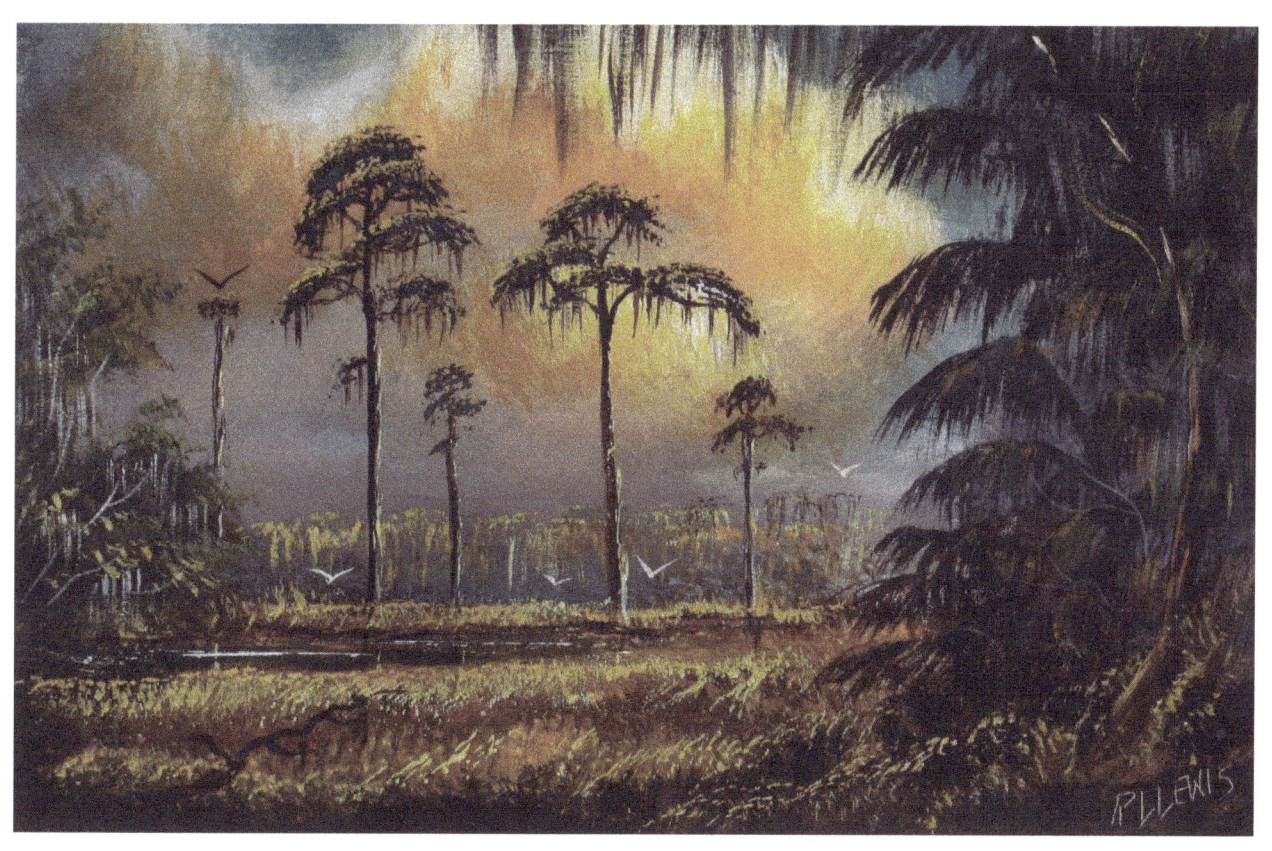

DID YOU KNOW:

RL often marvels at the explosion of colors that exist in Florida skies at the end of a very hot summer day.

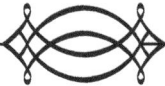

Pine Island on
The St. Johns River

Acrylic on Canvas, 36" x 24"

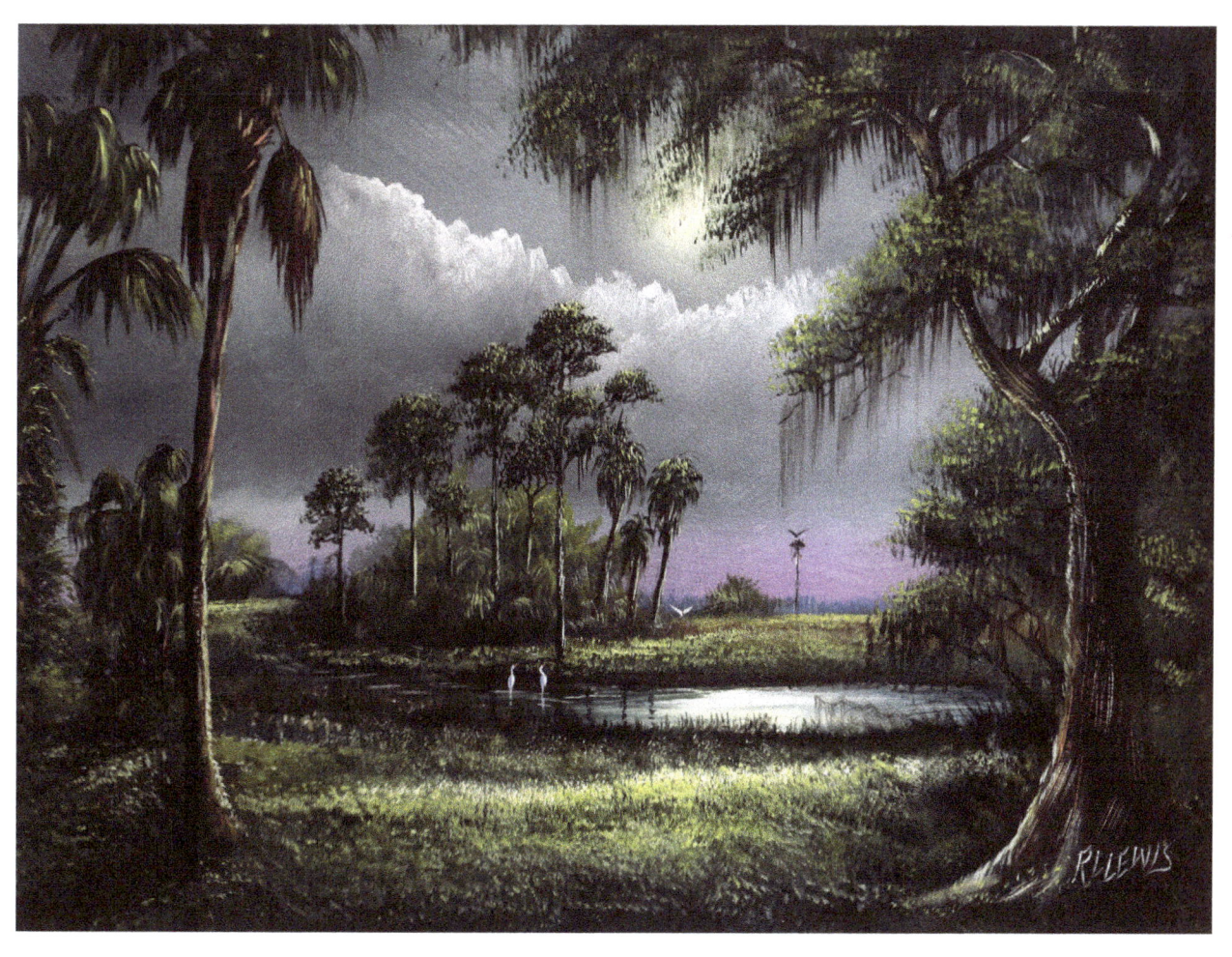

DID YOU KNOW:

*RL likes to paint landscapes that have
great metaphoric presence.*

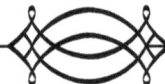

Pulpwood Harvesting in North Florida

Acrylic on Canvas, 30" x 24"

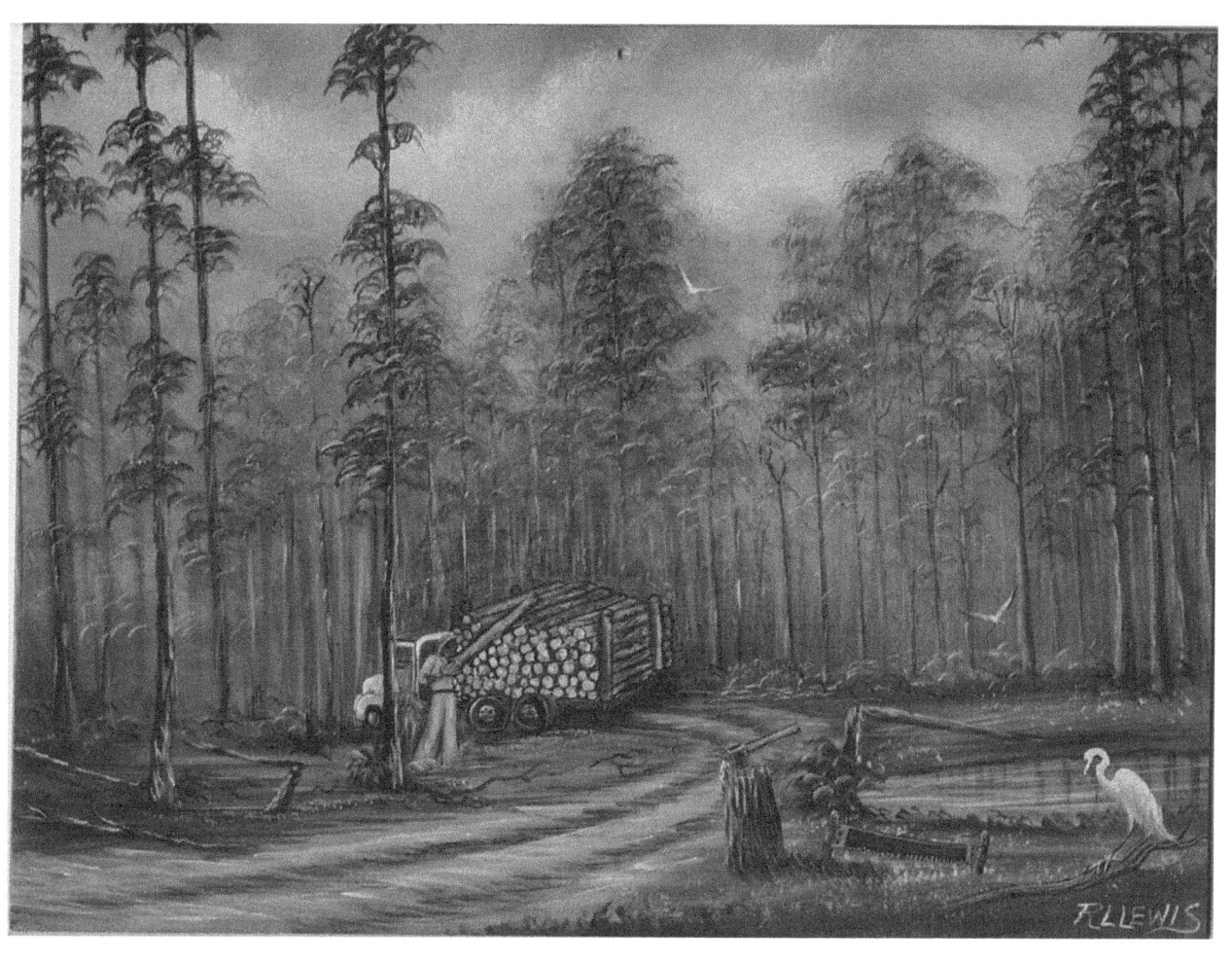

DID YOU KNOW:

RL's personal theme is, "To capture Florida as art history on canvas before it disappears!"

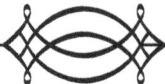

Tosohatchee State Reserve

Acrylic on Canvas, 30" x 24"

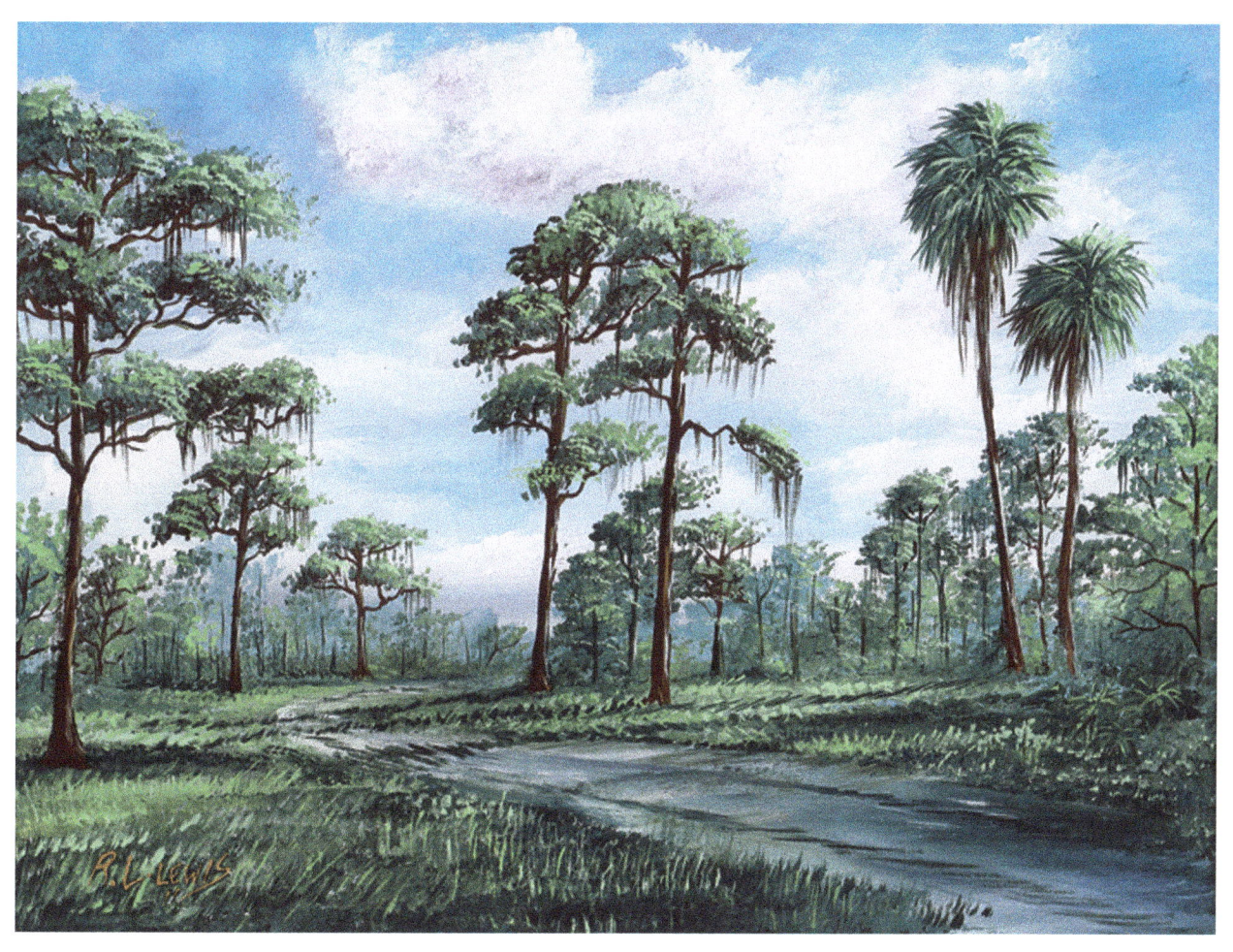

DID YOU KNOW:

RL thinks that,"It was very important to establish a repiore with his clientele. He states that for the most part, the relationships were more valuable to him than the actual sale of art."

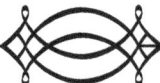

Late Afternoon At Tosohatchee State Reserve

Acrylic on Canvas, 36″ x 36″

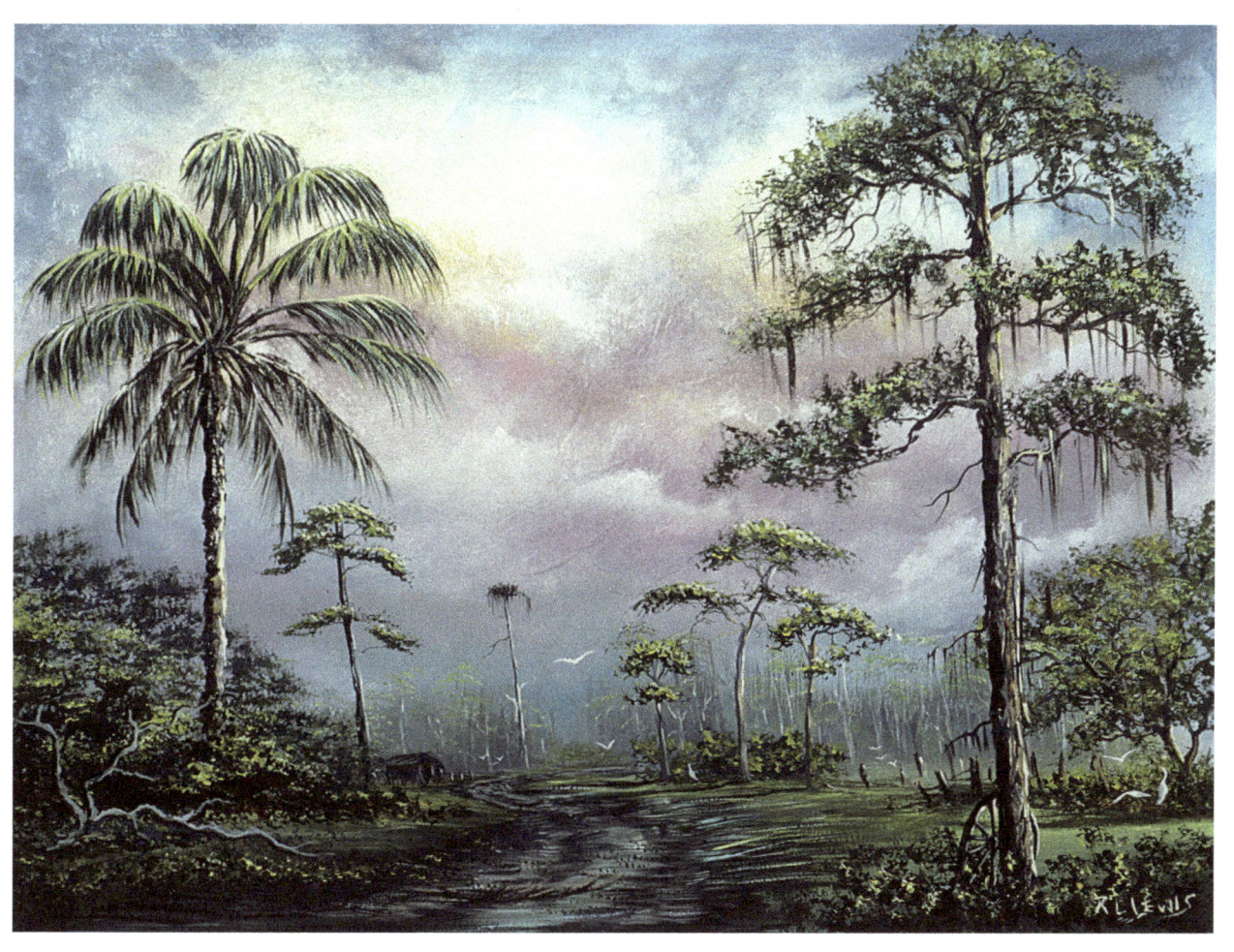

Did You Know:

Over the past twenty years, at his family's urging, RL has expanded his line of published pieces to include note cards, postcards, limited edition prints, instructional dvd's, mousepads and calendars.

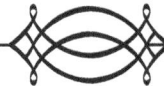

TRAILBLAZING ON THE ST. JOHNS RIVER

Acrylic on Canvas, 24" x 18"

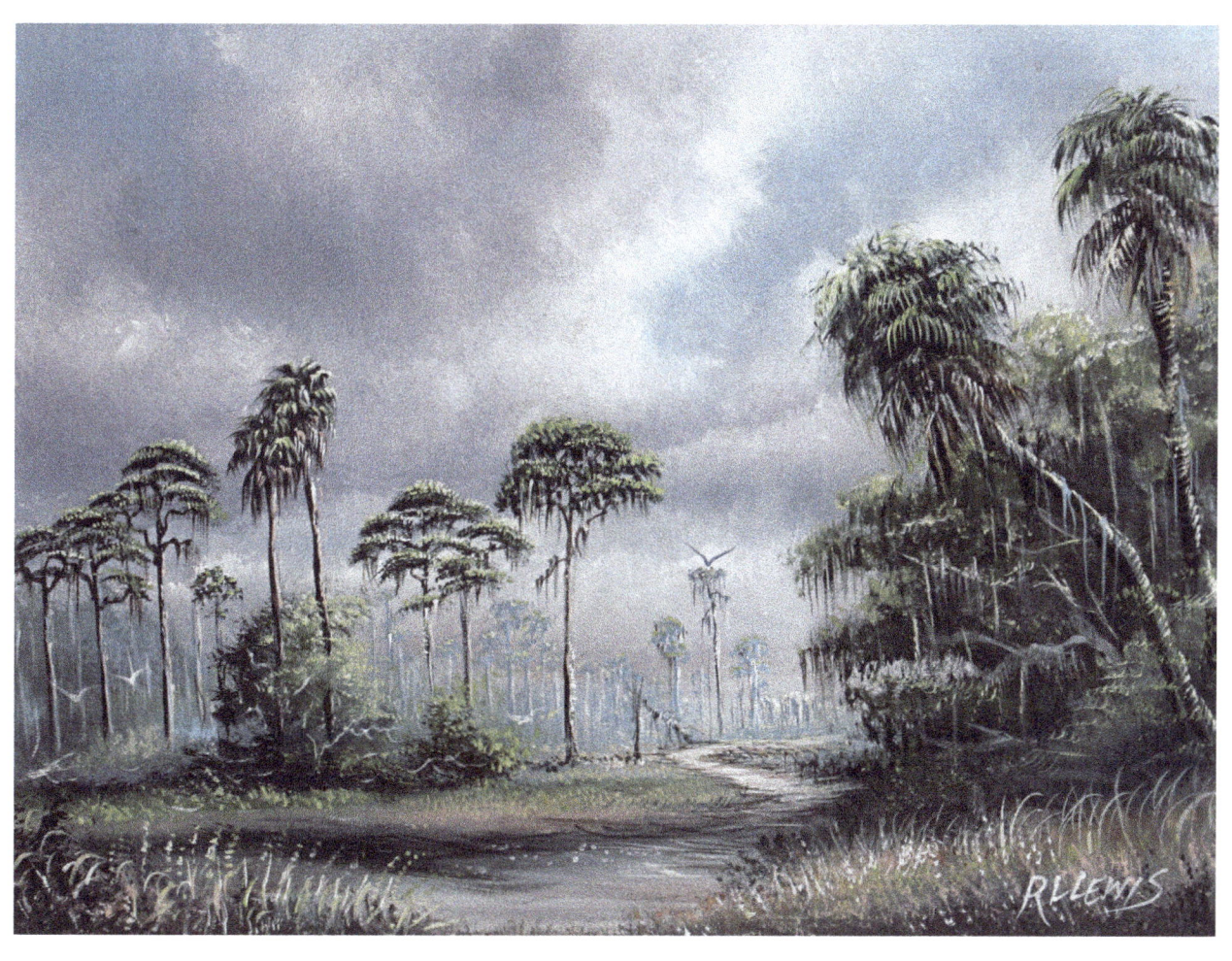

Did You Know:

RL preferred to paint with oils earlier in his painting career but he has painted with equal proficiency with acrylic in recent years.

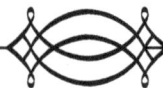

The Columbian exchange of the 15th and 16th

centuries is largely responsible for Botanical trees

like the Royal Poinciana, Jacaranda,

and Tabebuia Trees being in the Americas.

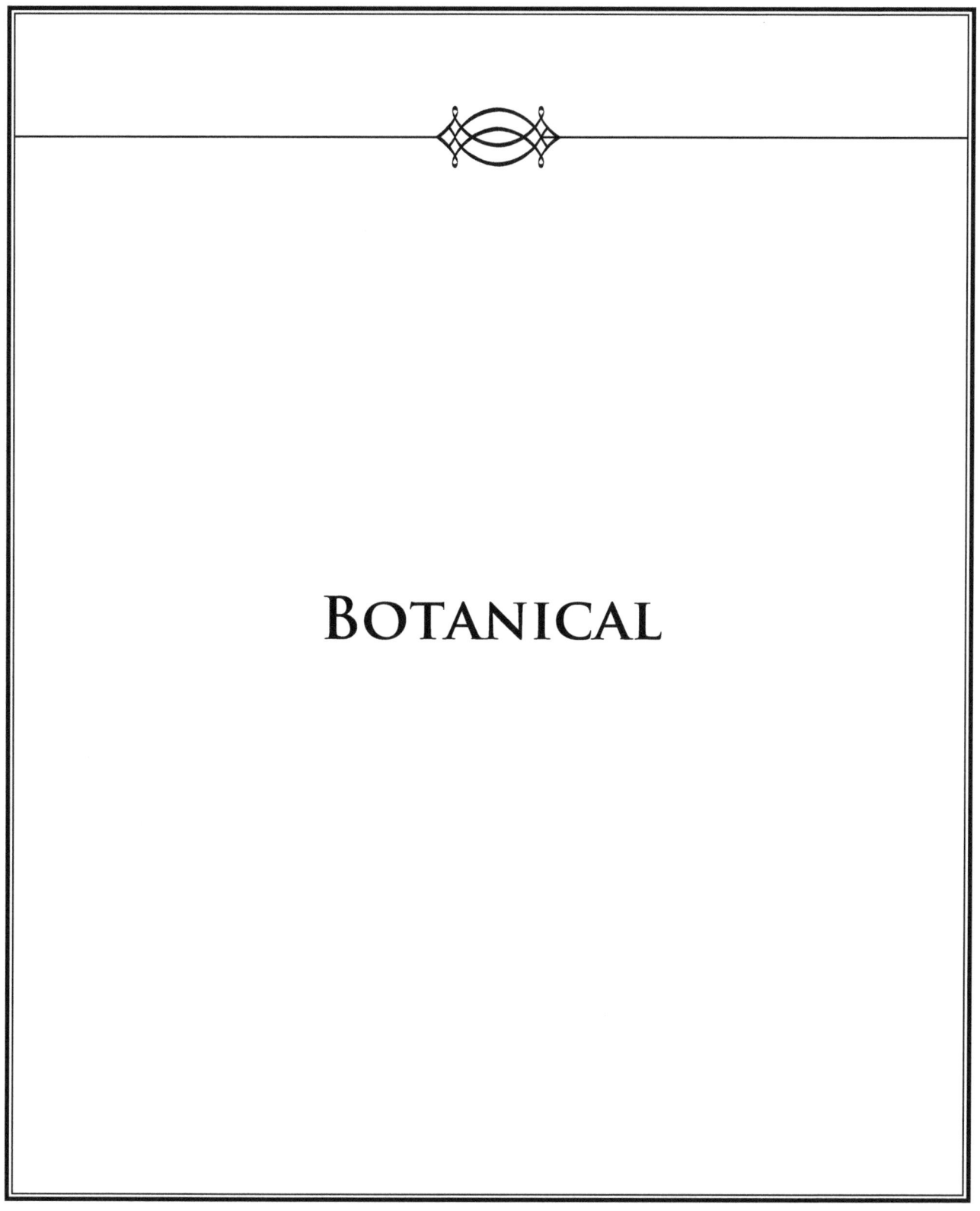

BOTANICAL

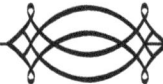

OLD SCHOOL VIRGINIA KEY
CIRCA 1950S
KEY BISCAYNE, FL

Mixed Media on Canvas, 36" x 24"

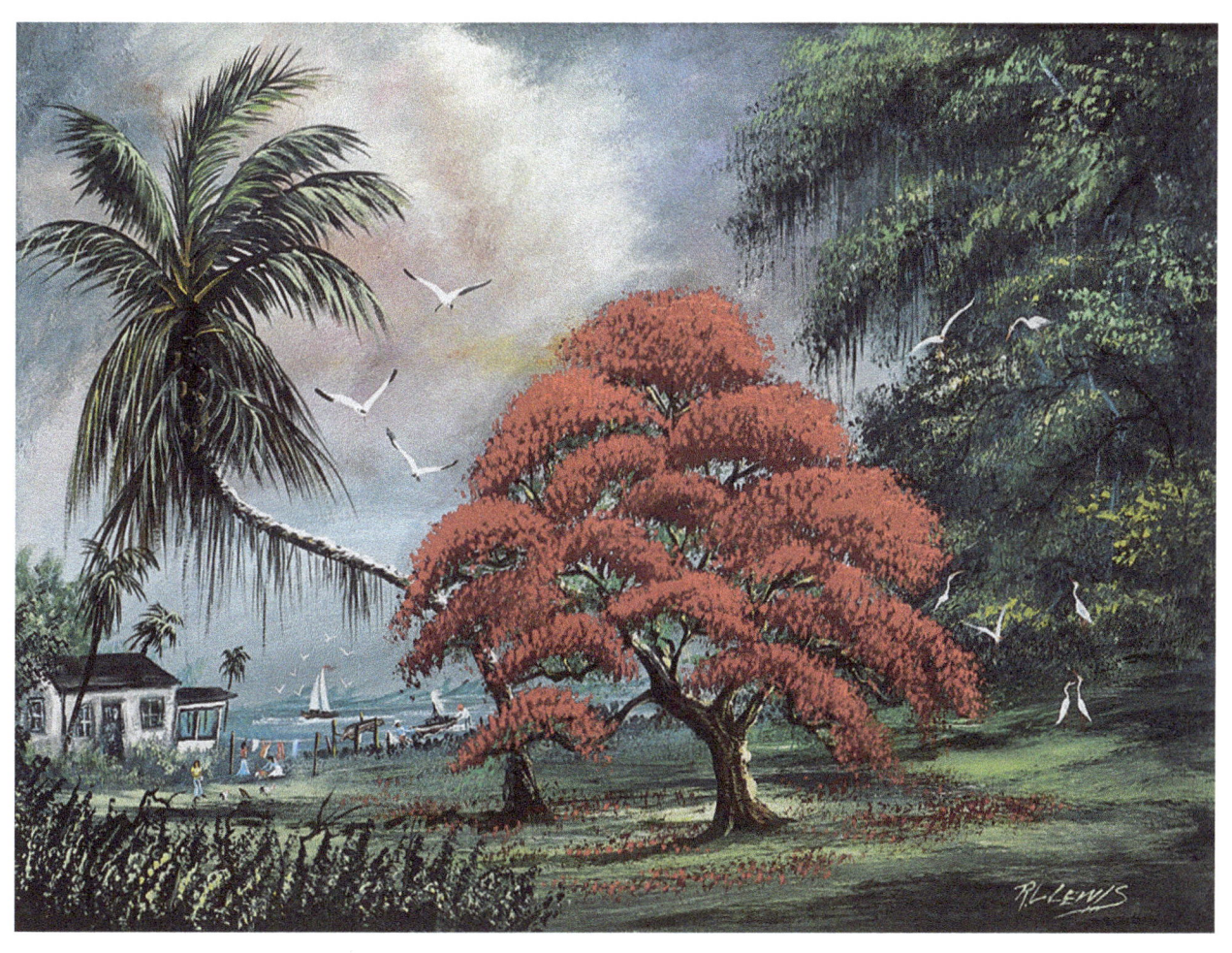

DID YOU KNOW:

Many clients look at the Royal Poinciana tree paintings as the signature landscape amongst the original highwaymen artist.

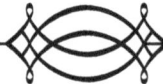

Arbor of Purple Bougainvilla at Cypress Gardens Circa 1970

Acrylic on Canvas, 20" x 16"

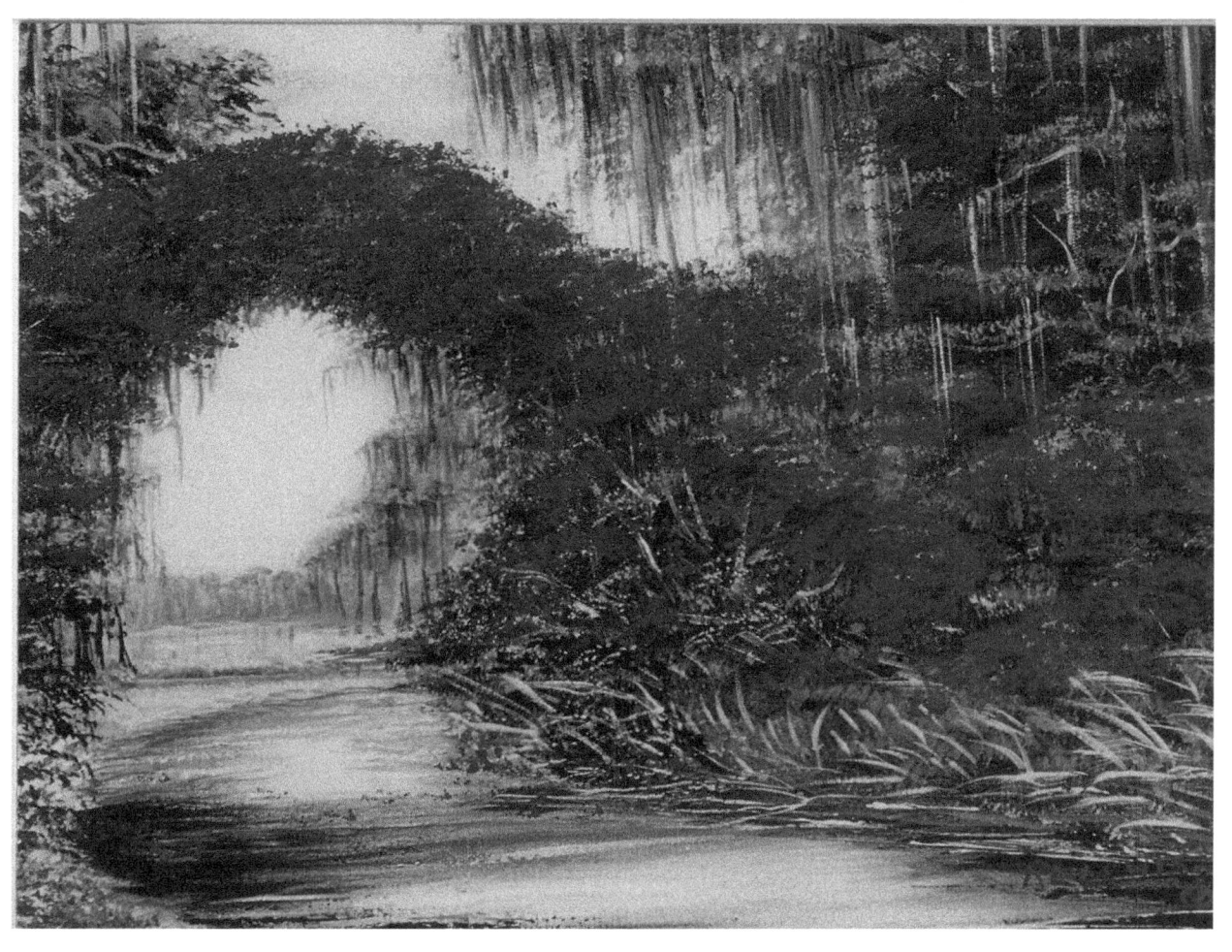

Did You Know:

RL believes that the Highwaymen class of artist will be remembered in history like the Hudson river school of artists, America's first group of landscape painters.

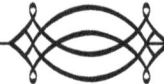

Flamboyant in Bloom During the Rainy Season

Mixed Media on Masonite, 36" x 24"

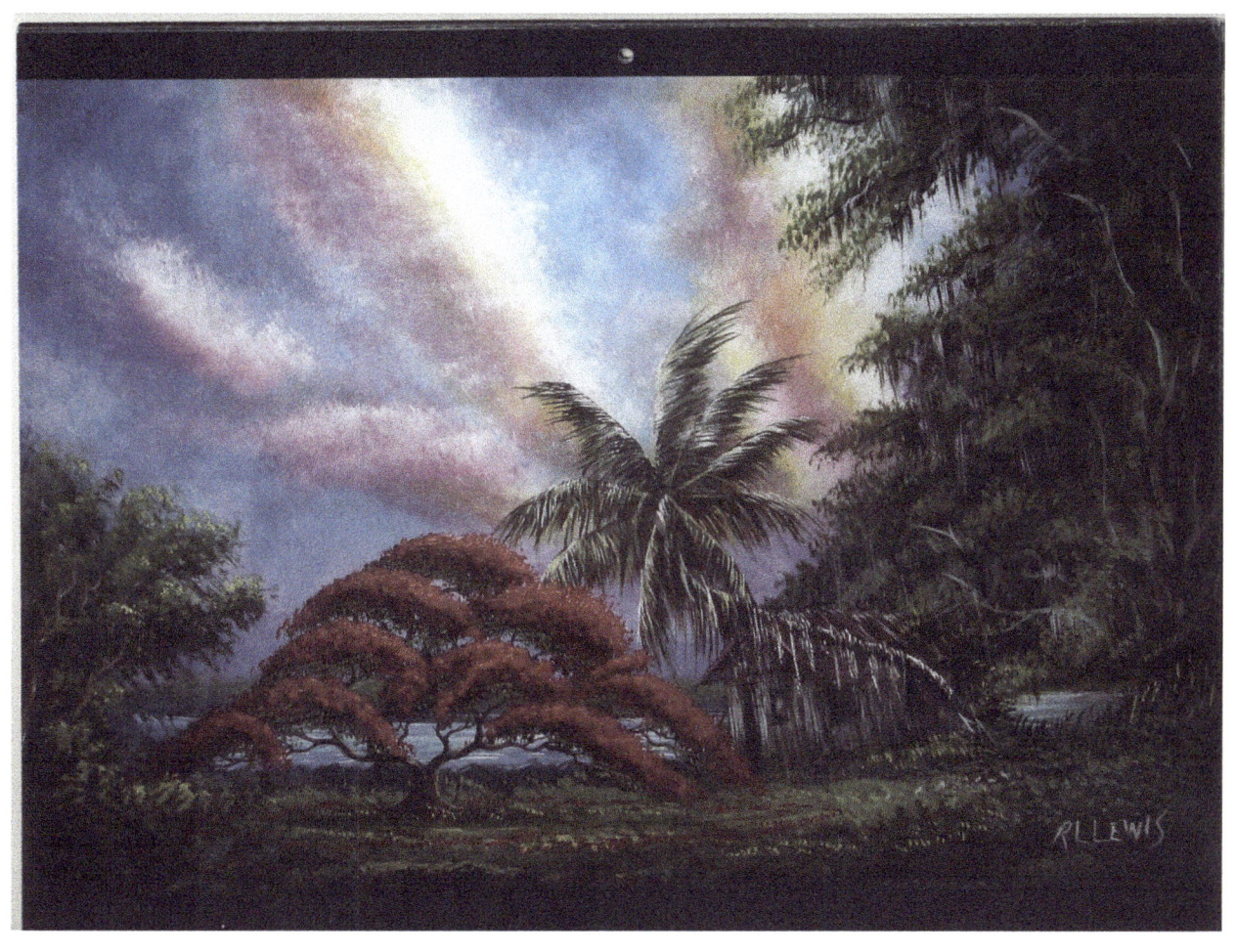

DID YOU KNOW:

RL denotes that, "You can't paint exactly everything that you see in many landscapes, because it may become muddled and make a client less likely to purchase the painting!"

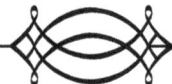

Jacaranda in Bloom

Acrylic on Canvas, 20" x 16"

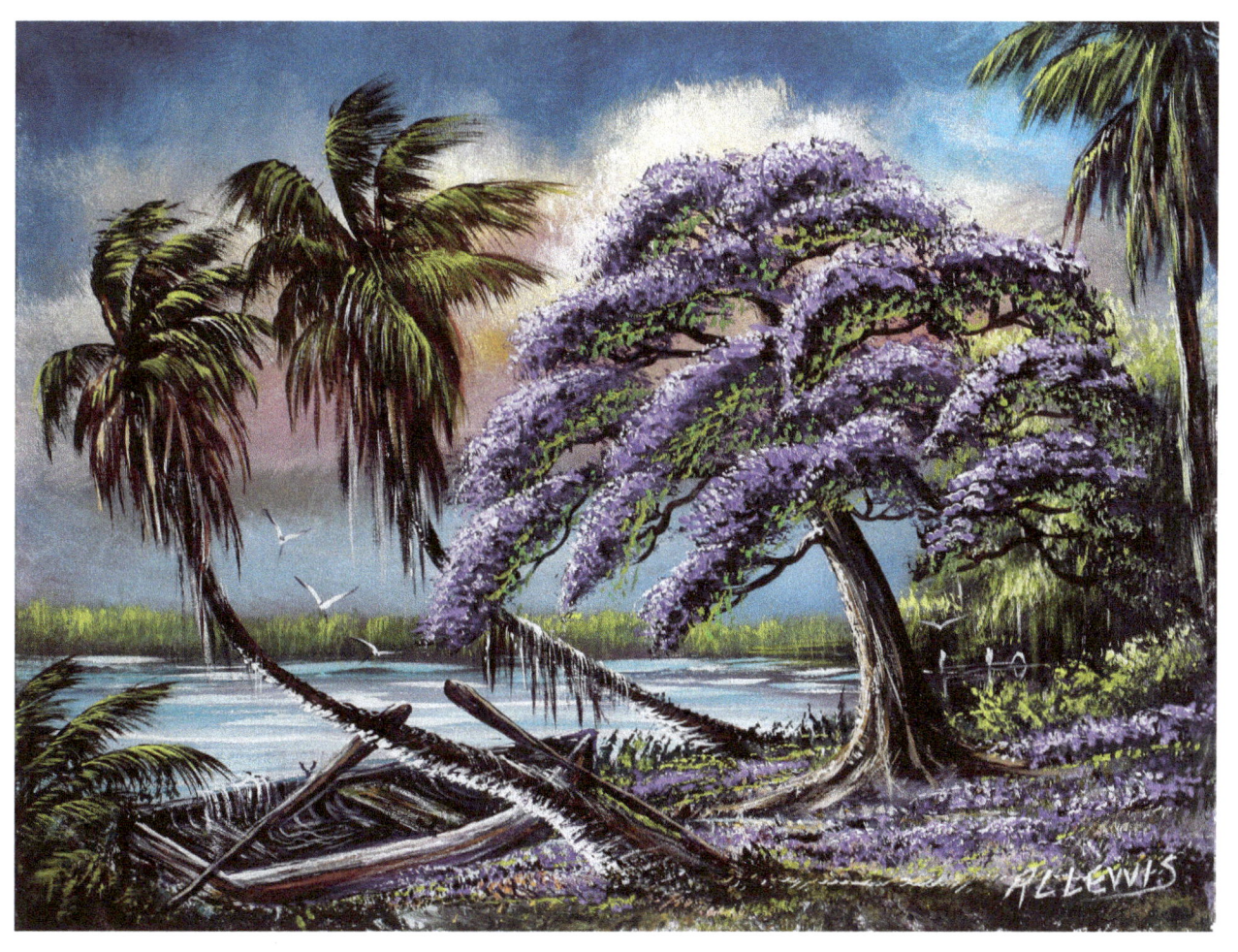

DID YOU KNOW:

The jacaranda tree is also called the "lavender blue tree." It largely grows in the tropical and subtropical regions of Florida. It typically blooms in the Spring and early Summer in Florida.

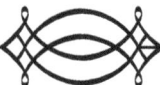

RL is very well known for his paintings of

Florida Orange Groves. He often partners with

organizations like the Florida Gift Fruit Shippers

Association to help bring attention to the industry.

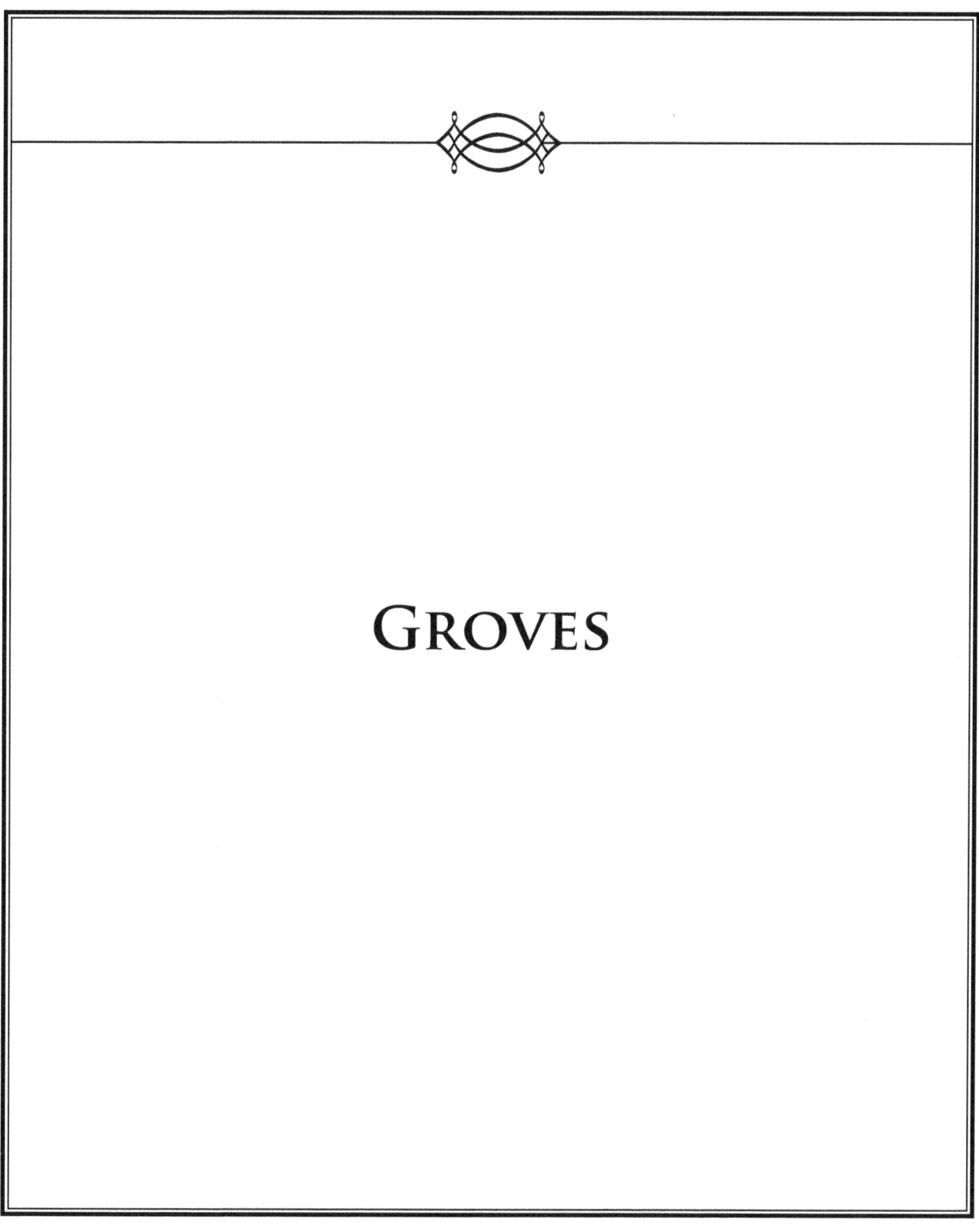

GROVES

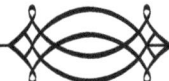

DAVENPORT, FLORIDA
ORANGE GROVE

Acrylic on Canvas, 24"x20"

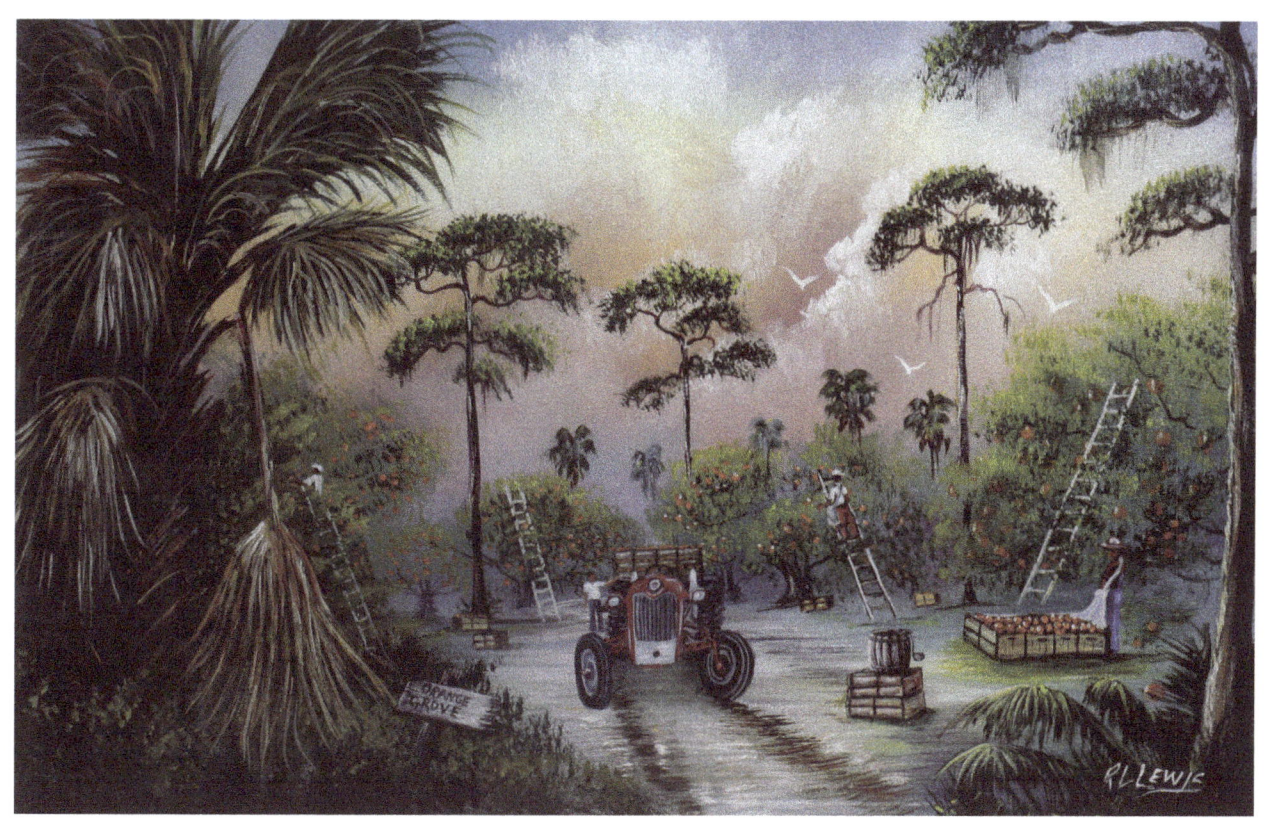

DID YOU KNOW:

RL paints Florida scenes that is quickly disappearing!

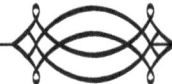

Morning Harvest

Oil on Canvas, 36″ x 24″

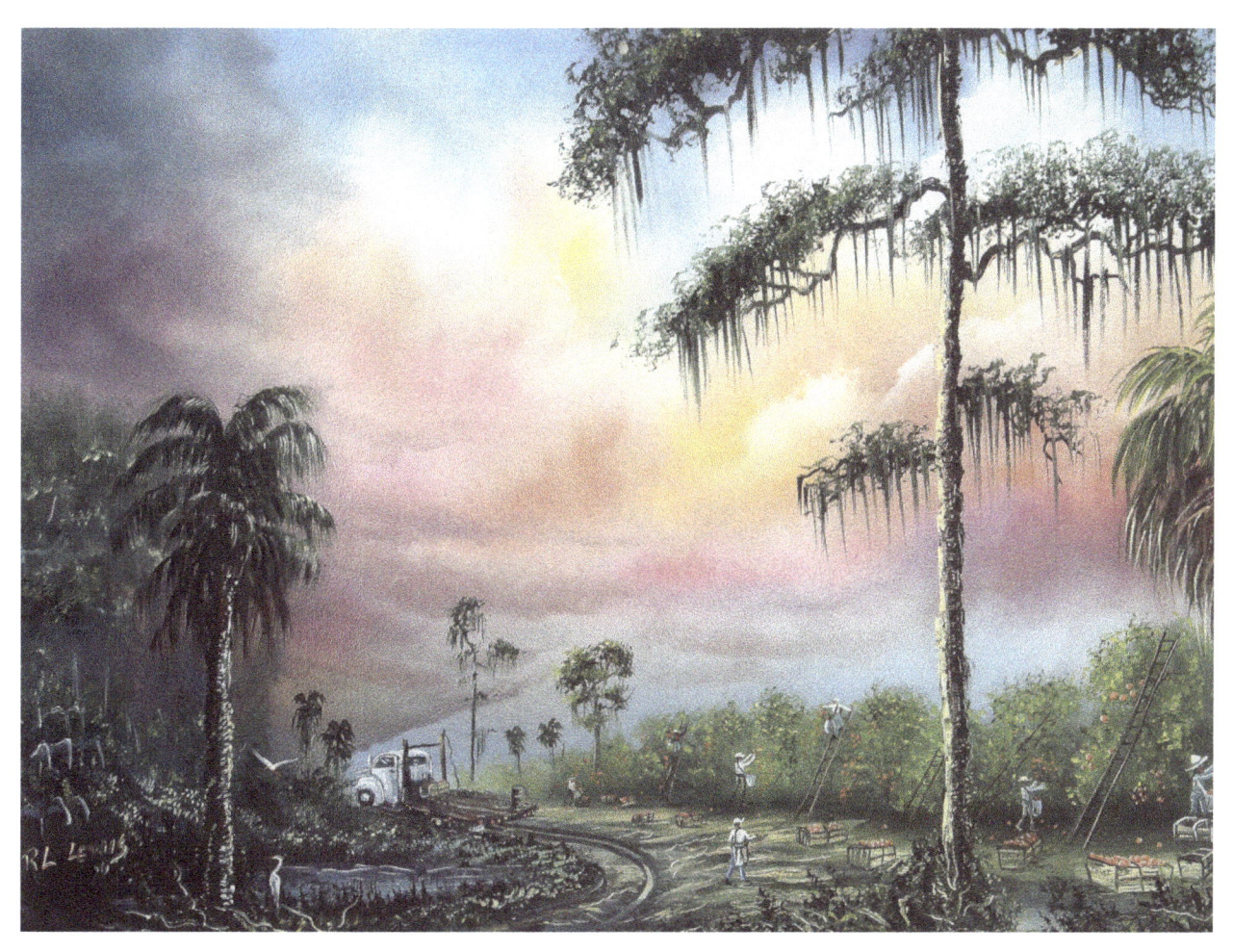

DID YOU KNOW:

RL enjoys painting the glorious colors of the Florida skies.

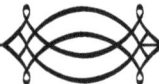

Orange Grove on the Ocklawaha River Conner, Fl

(near Palatka, Fl)
Circa 1902e

Acrylic on Canvas, 28" x 22"

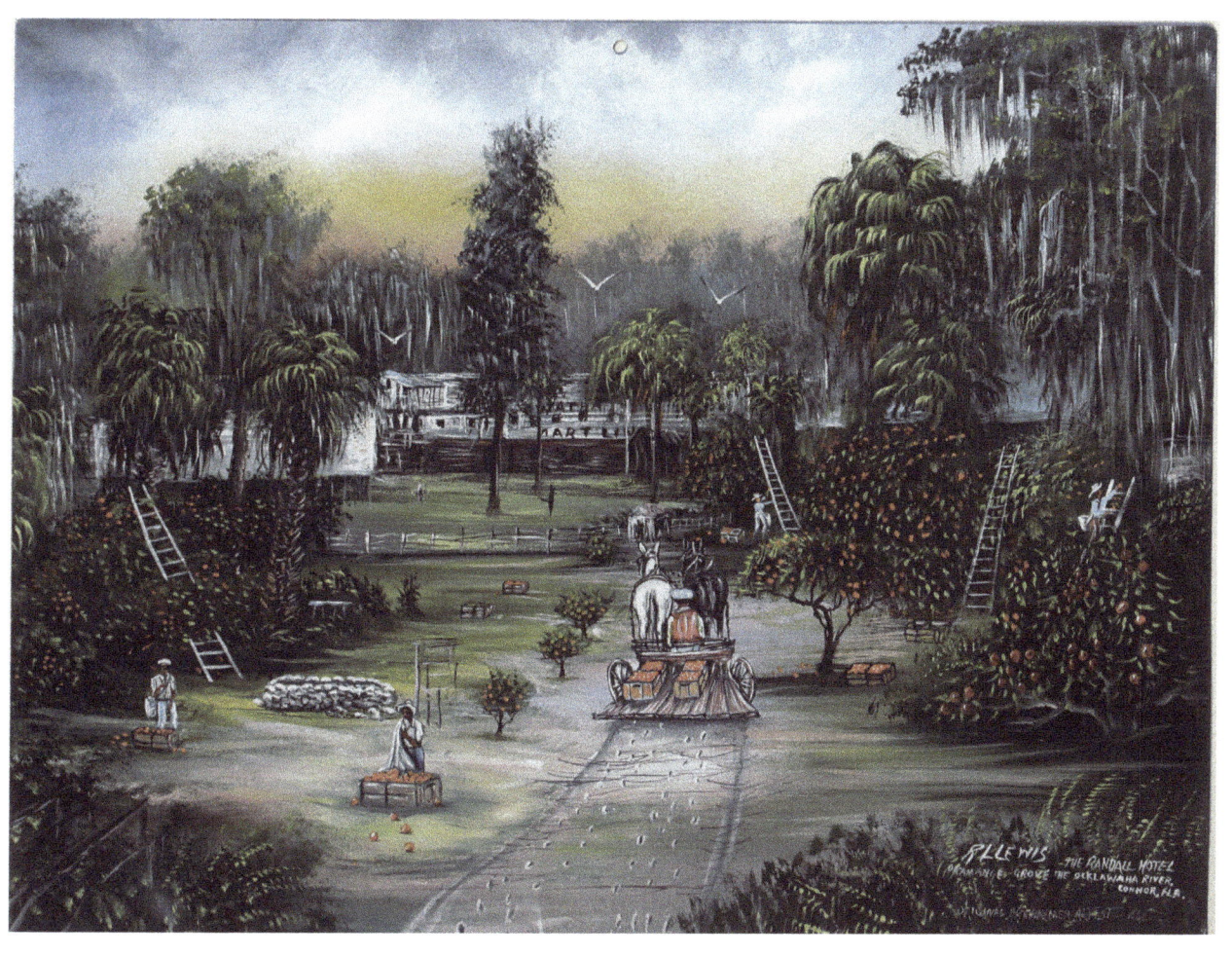

DID YOU KNOW:

The city of Palatka restored the historic hartline steamship for travel on the St. Johns River.

85

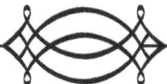

Nevin's Orange Grove
Circa 1950s

Acrylic on Canvas, 48" x 36"

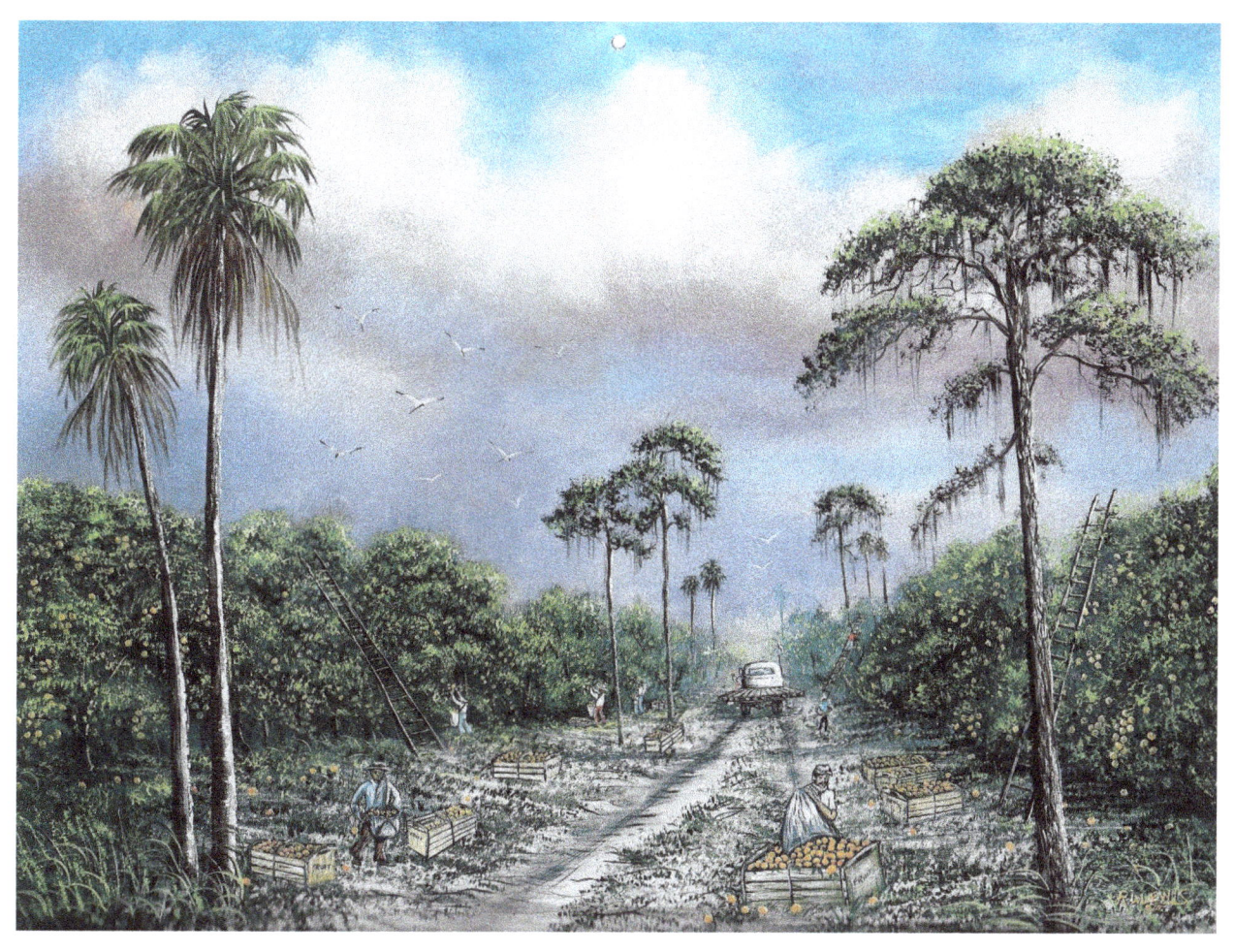

DID YOU KNOW:

In order to make extra money as a teenager during the Christmas season, RL would work in orange groves, such as the one in this scene that contained lots of afternoon life and activity.

As a teenager, along with his brothers, RL remembers having to help his father build and cultivate a small orange grove in City Point, Florida (north of Cocoa, where his family had moved during his adolescent years.)

87

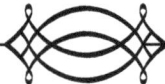

RL thinks that Florida's Lakes and Rivers are to be

treasured and at all cost preserved for

future generations to enjoy!

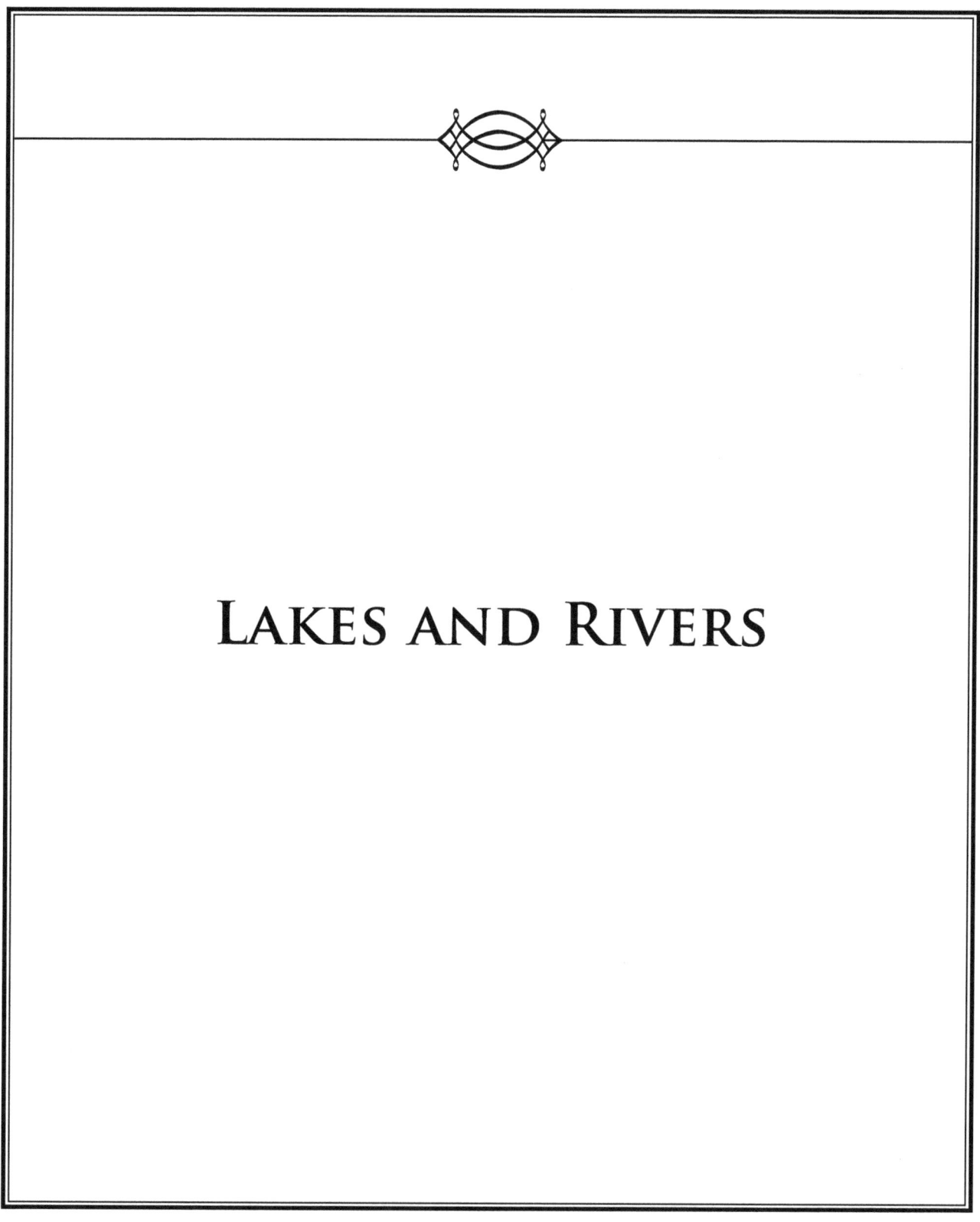

LAKES AND RIVERS

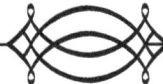

First in Flight, Banana River
Merrit Island, FL

Mixed Media, 60" x 48"

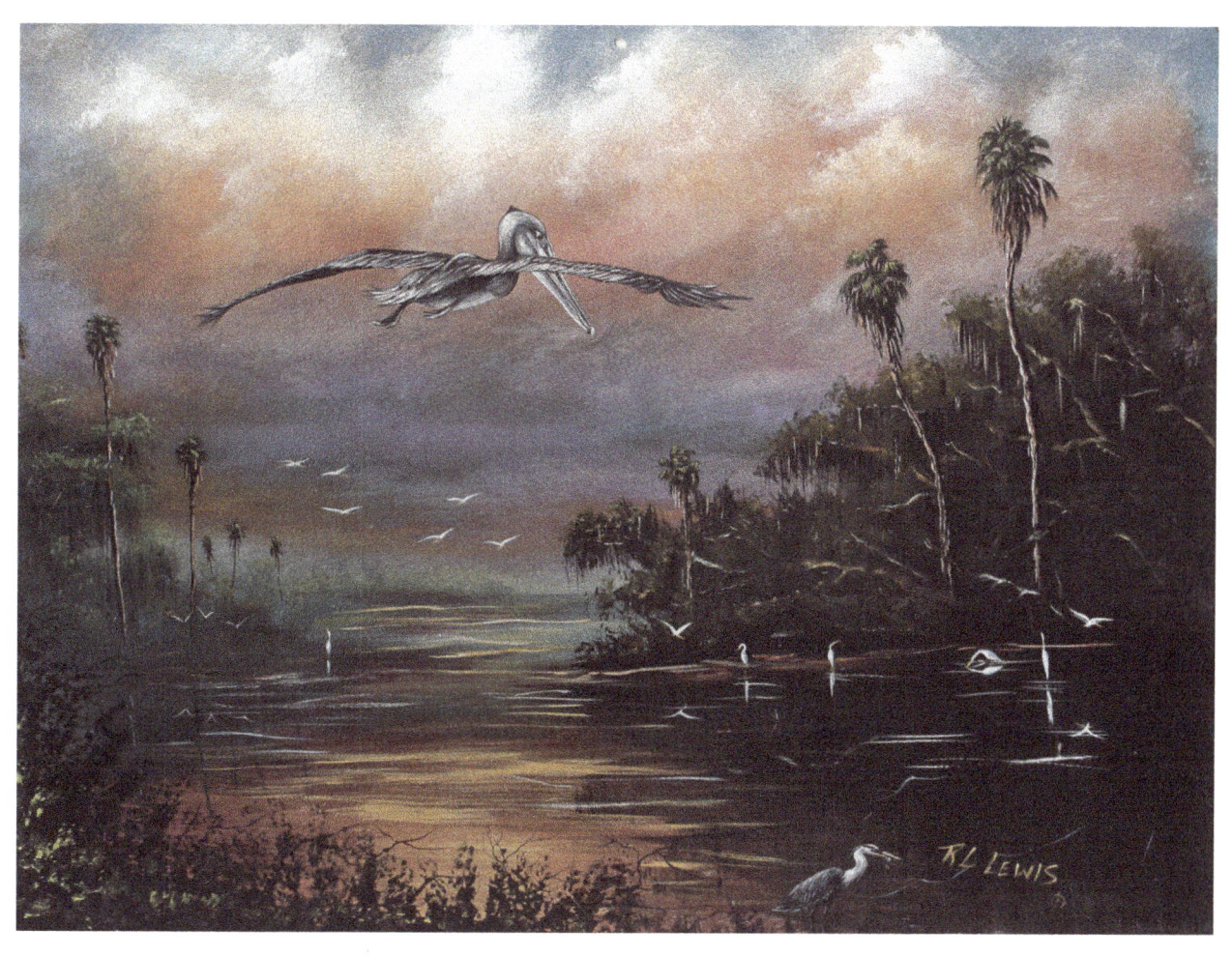

DID YOU KNOW:

"I enjoy painting Banana River scenes. This river system is also called A Thousand Islands."

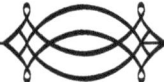

A Whitetail Buck Peering Out on Shingle Creek – Headwaters to the Florida Everglades
Orlando, FL

Acrylic on Stretch Canvas
24" x 12"

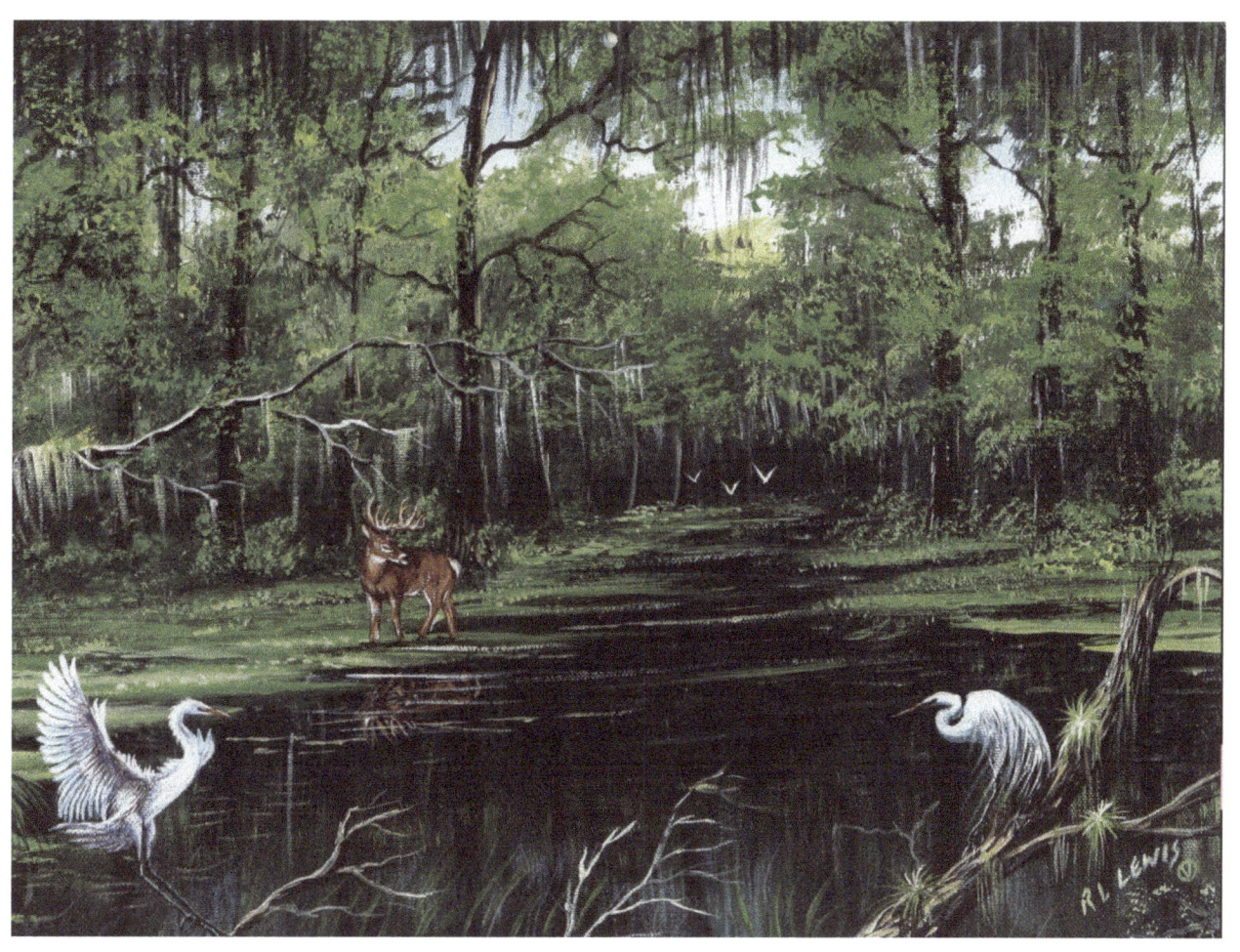

DID YOU KNOW:

RL notes that many hunters come to him requesting to have their prized Whitetail Buck painted.

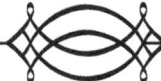

Indian River Lagoon Sunrise
Cocoa, FL
Circa 1968

Oil on Upson Board

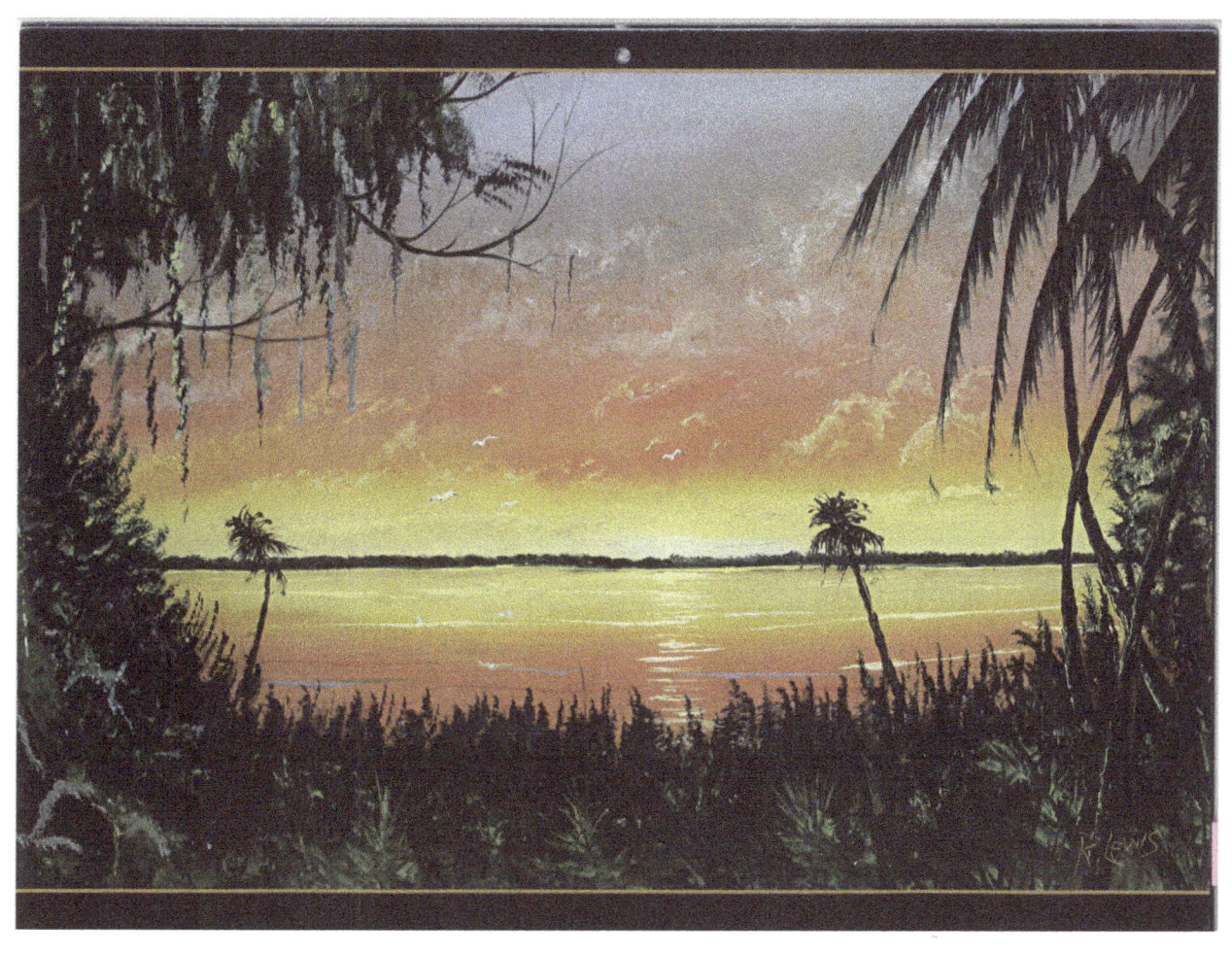

DID YOU KNOW:

*RL sold many paintings to clients during 1968. He considers
this year a break through time for him as
a Florida landscape artist.*

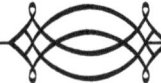

Indian River Lagoon Sunrise
Cocoa, FL
Circa 1970

Acrylic on Upson Board, 20" x 16"

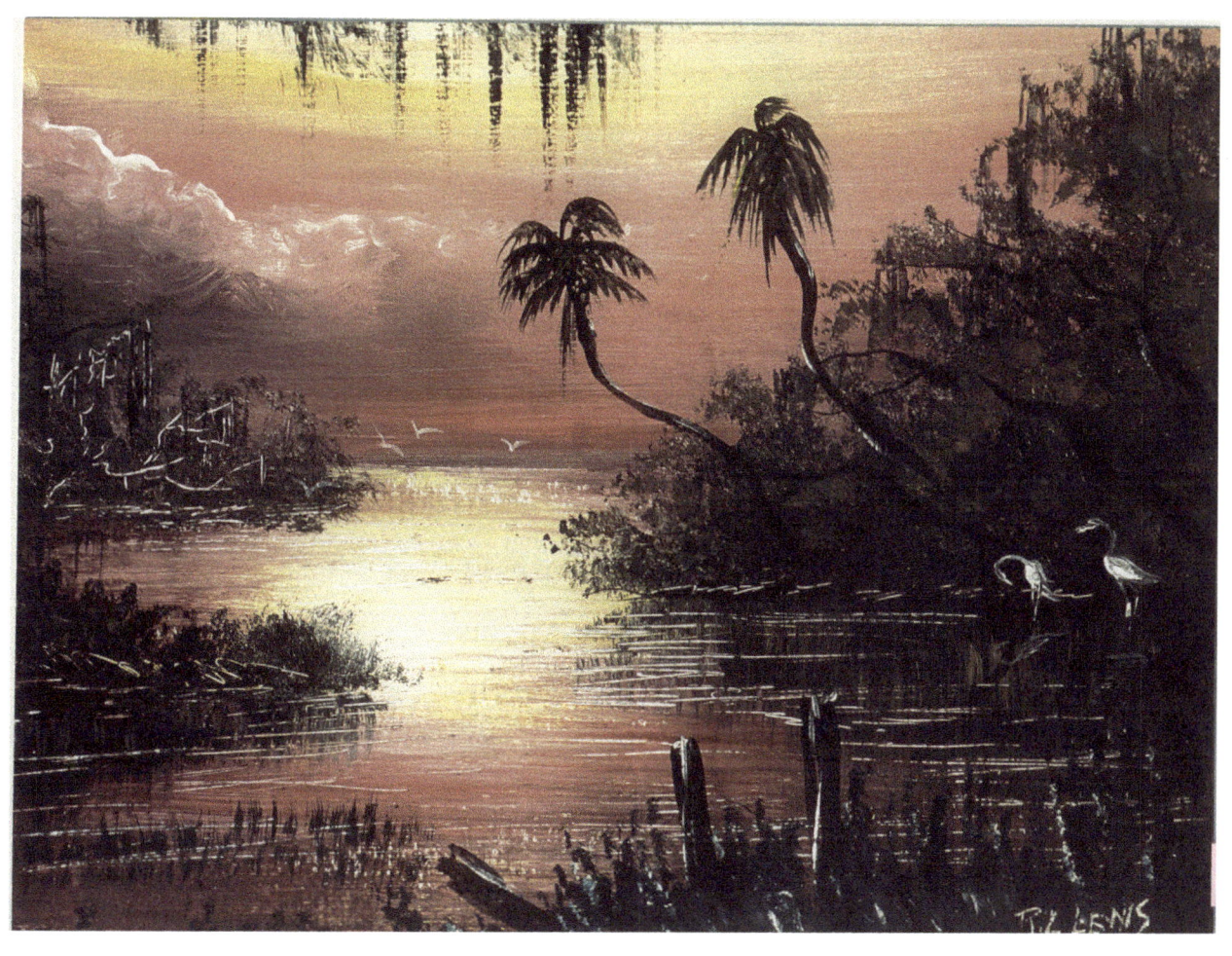

DID YOU KNOW:

RL began migrating to canvas panels and stretch canvas in the mid-1970s.

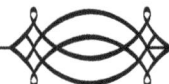

Istokpoga River Sunset

Mixed Media on Canvas, 36" x 24"

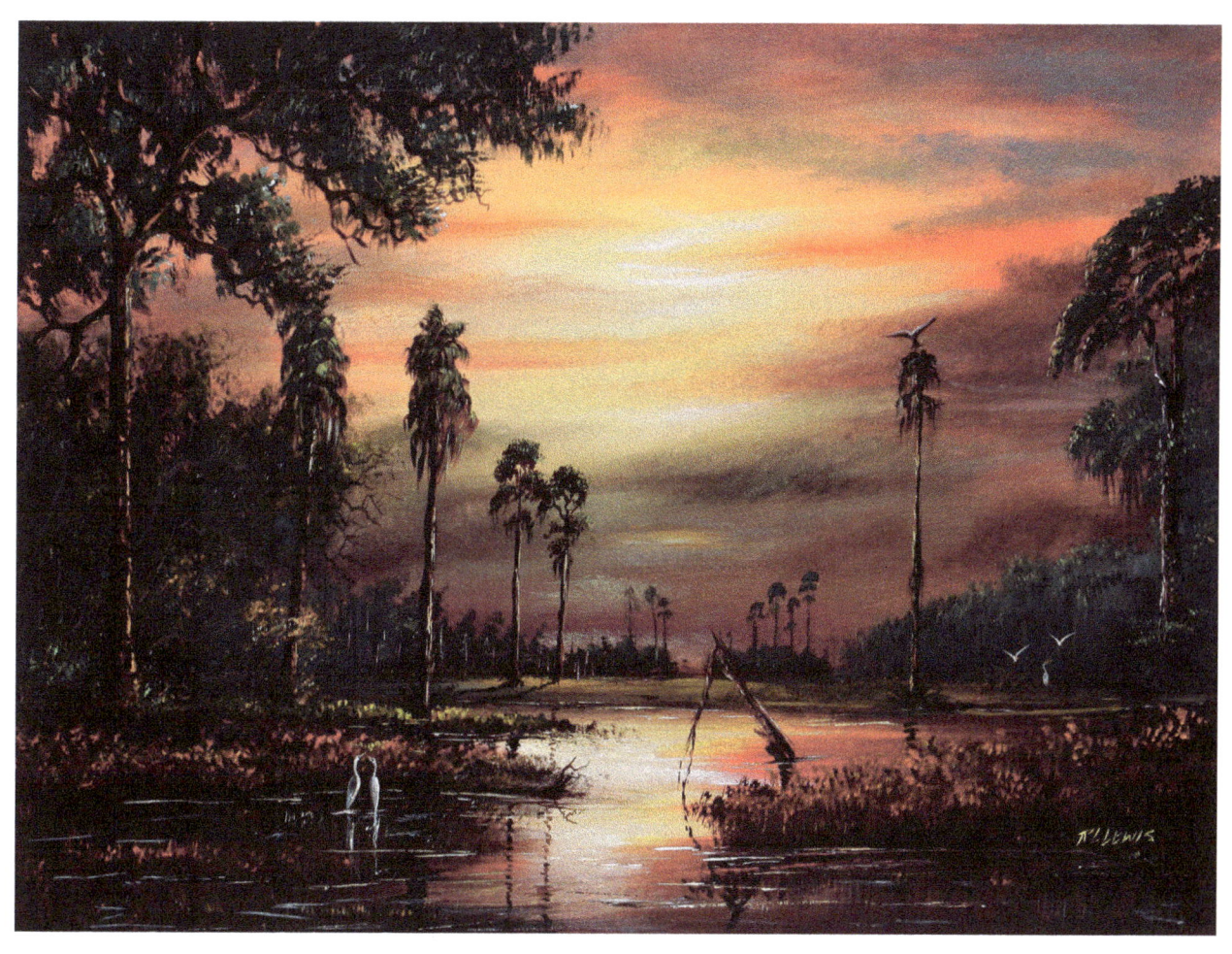

DID YOU KNOW:

The Istokpoga is the 5th largest river in the state of Florida, as it feeds into both Lake Okeechobee and Kissimmee River.

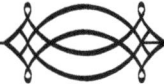

Lake Beresford, headwaters to the St. Johns River in Deland, Fl

Acrylic on Canvas, 20" x 16"

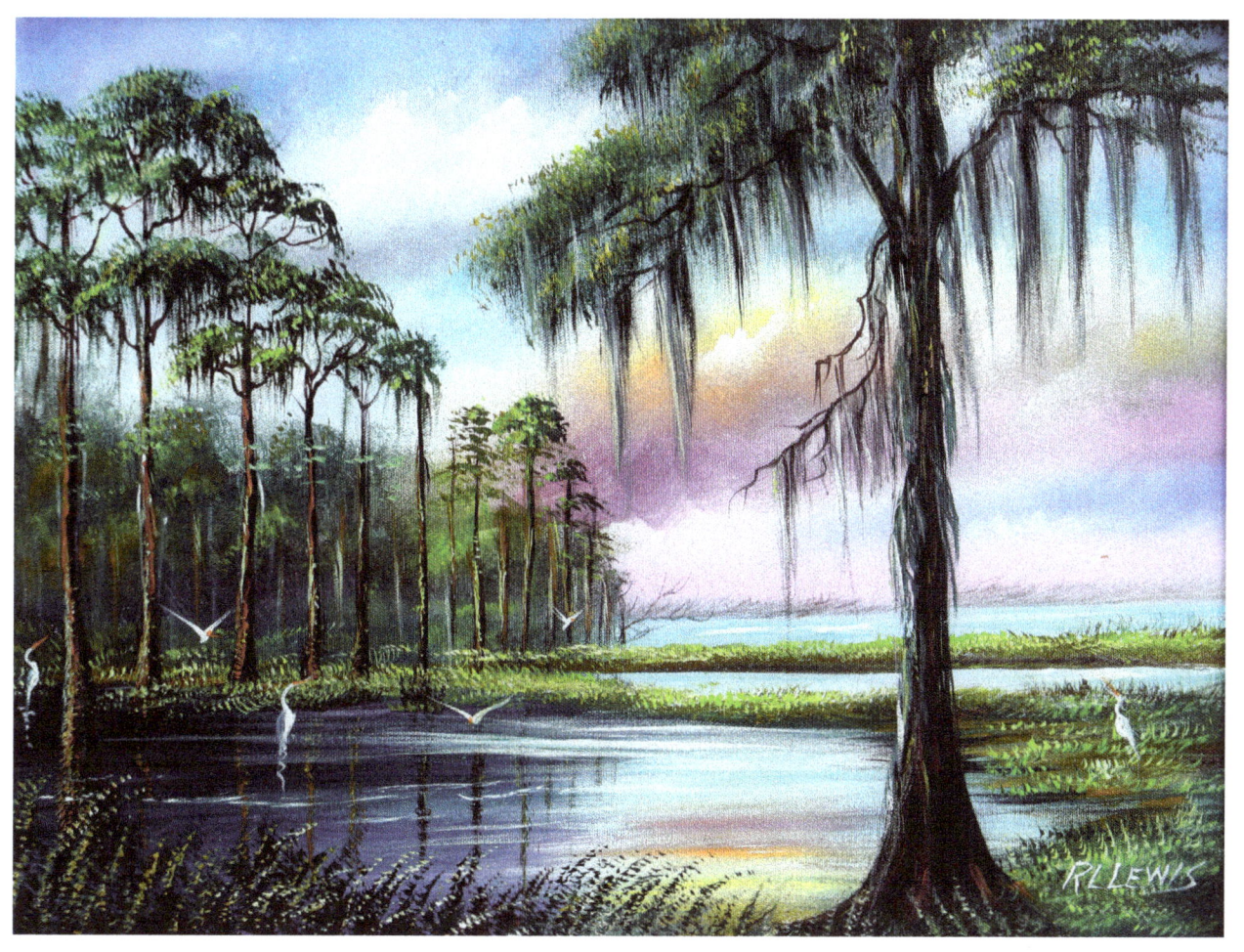

DID YOU KNOW:

RL has in past times considered himself more of an impressionistic artist. nevertheless, he is quick to note that because of his ability to "paint beyond his trademark Florida landscapes—he prefers to call himself just a balanced artist."

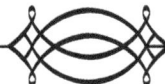

Moonlight on the Indian River Lagoon Circa 1974

Oil on Knapsack, 20" x 16"

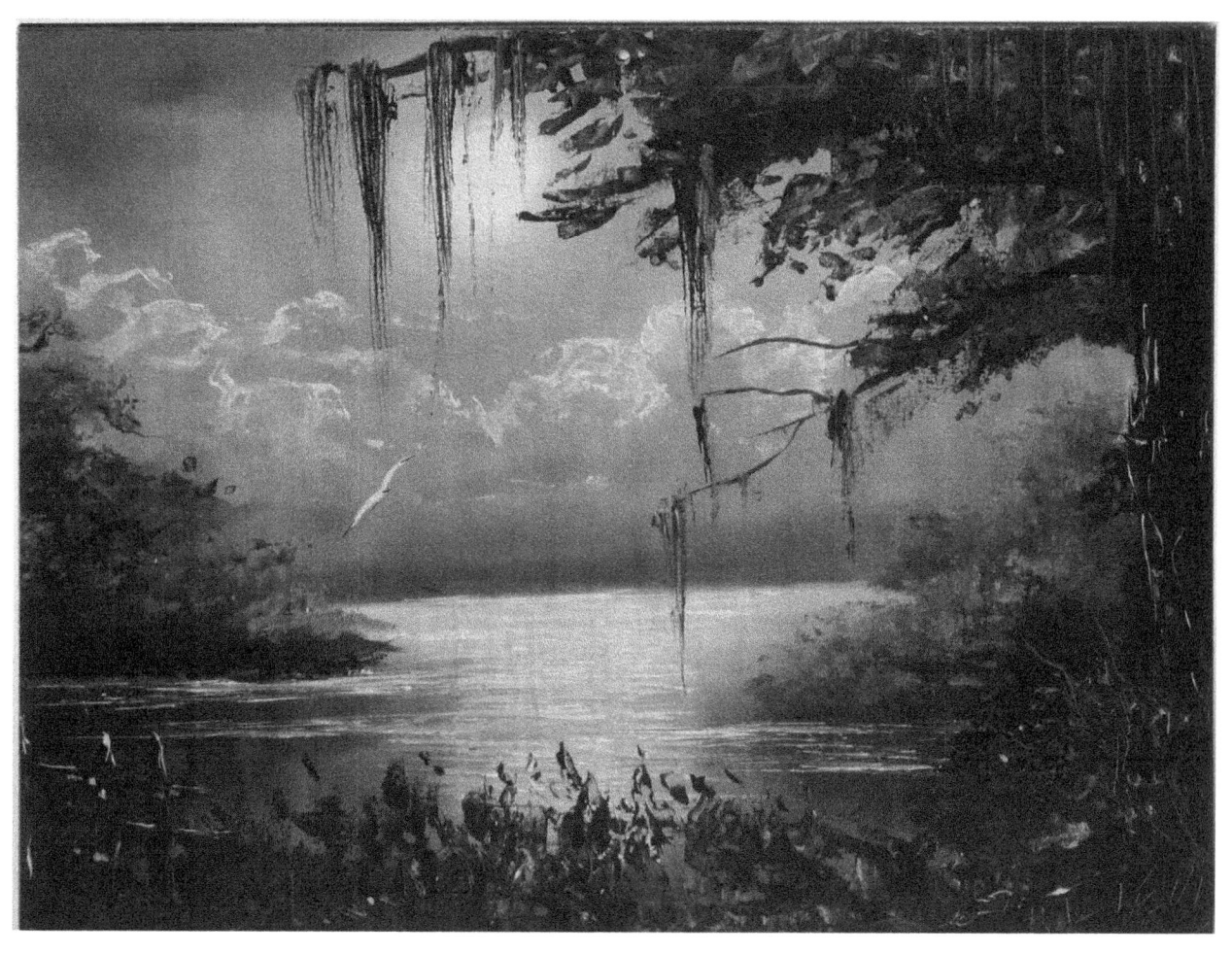

DID YOU KNOW:

The Indian River Lagoon was RL Lewis' playground as a kid.

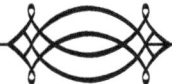

Morning on the St. Johns River

Oil on Canvas, 28" x 22"

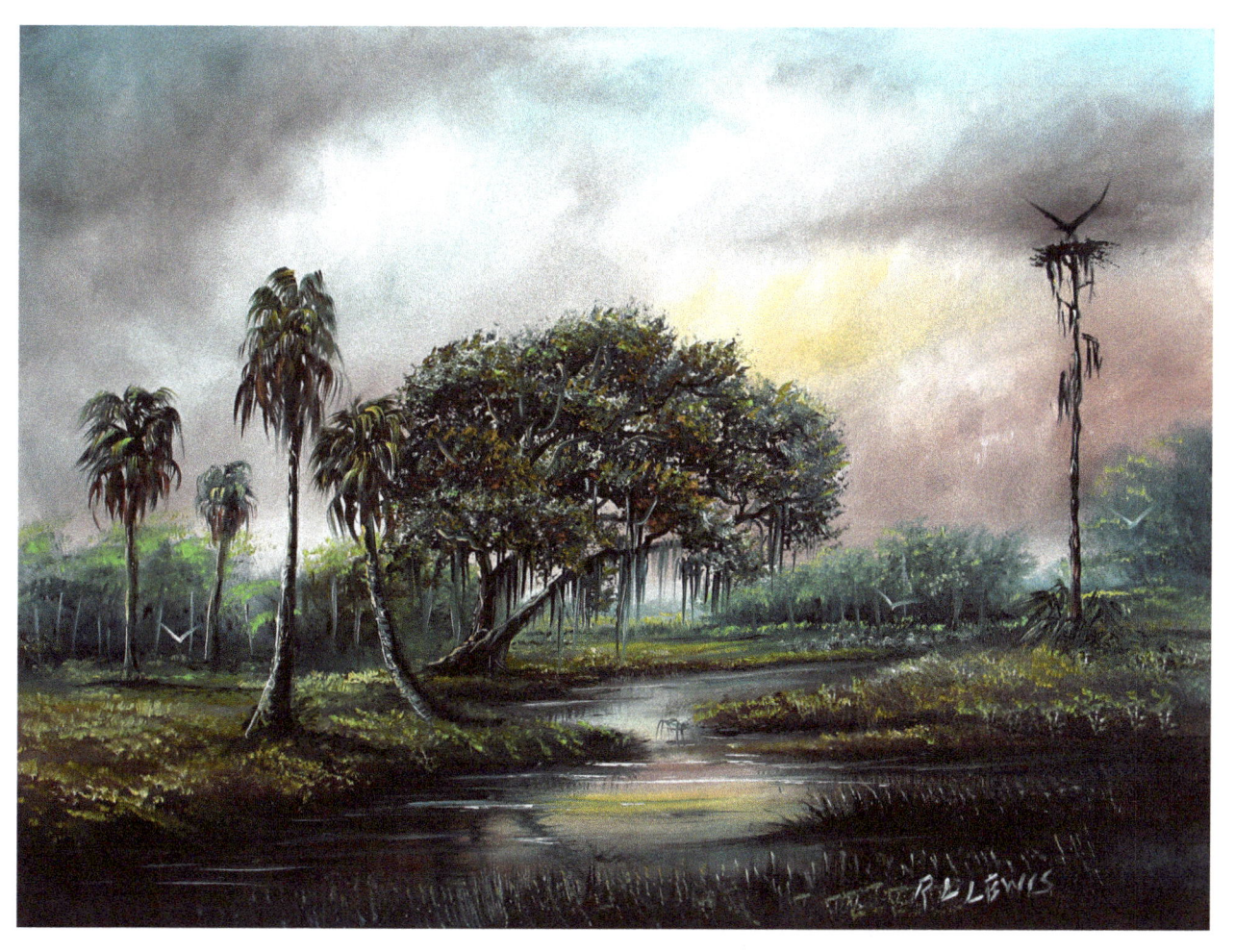

DID YOU KNOW:

RL has painted many St. Johns River scenes for various clients over many years.

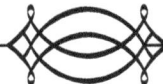

A Great White Egret's View of the Loxahatchee River Palm Beach County, Fl

Oil on Canvas, 24" x 18"

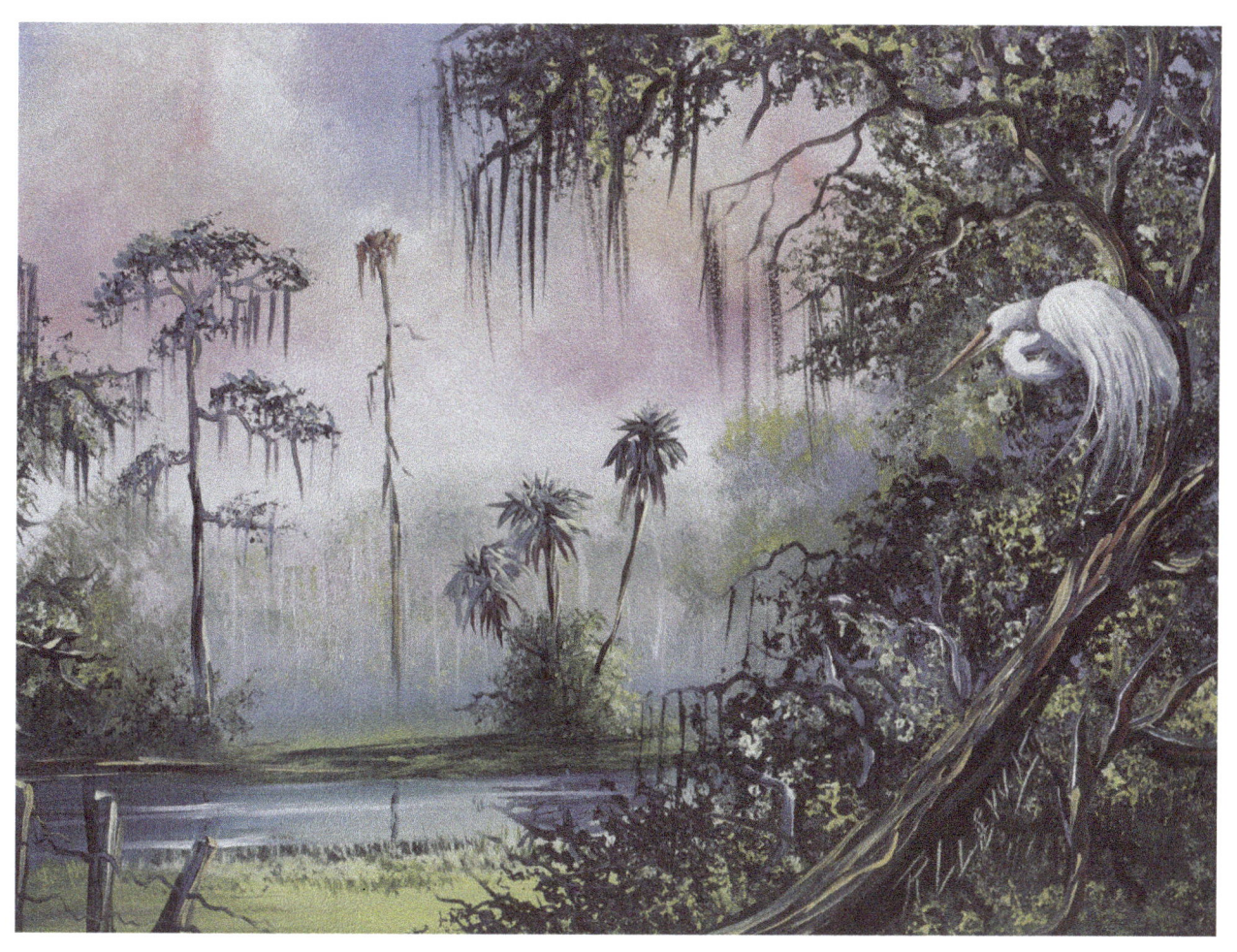

DID YOU KNOW:

*RL points out that an artist has arrived when
he is not afraid to use color.*

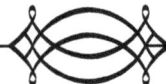

Old School
New Smyrna Beach Inlet
Circa 1970s

Oil on Canvas, 36" x 24"

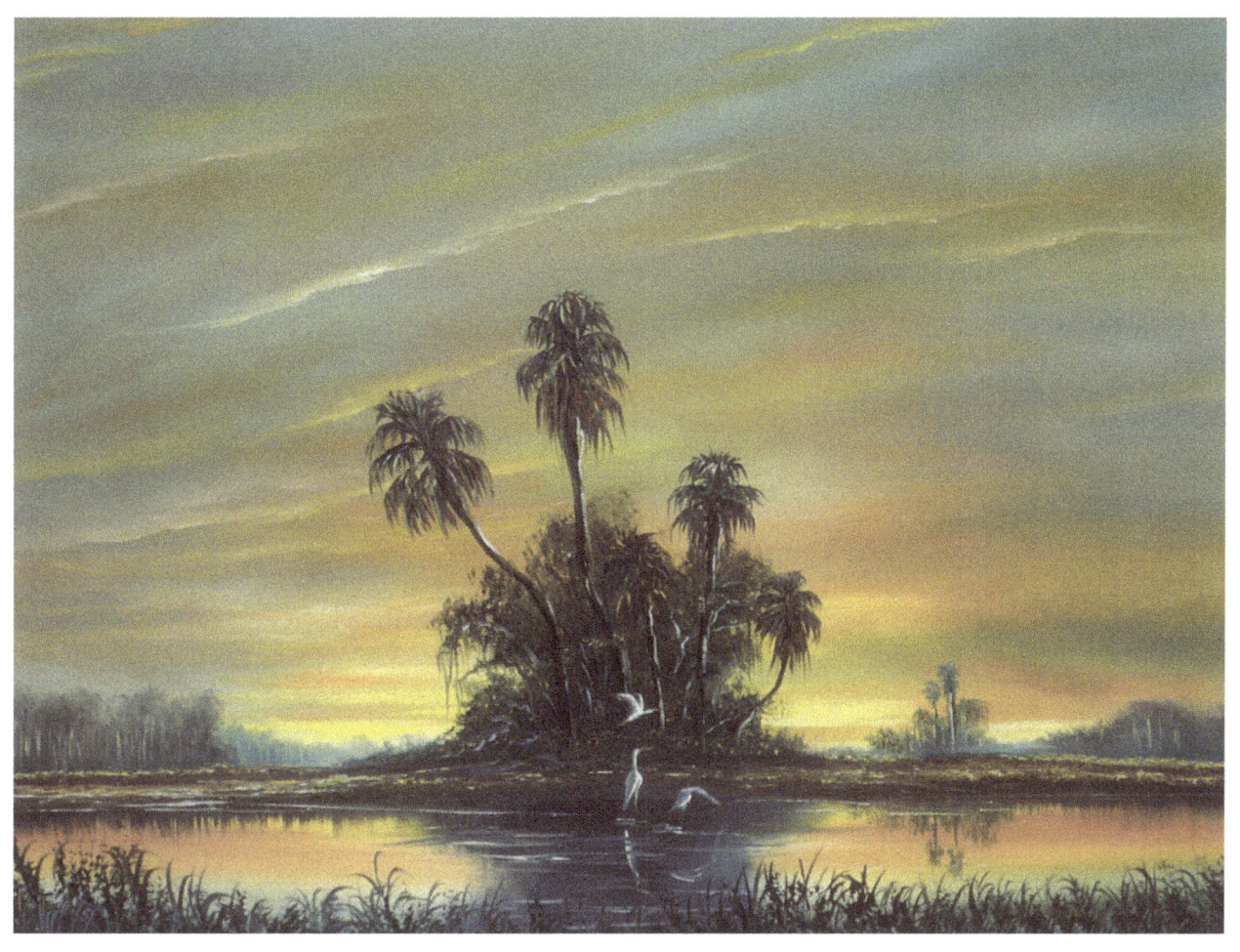

DID YOU KNOW:

According to Lewis, "I always expected to improve as an artist with each painting. I believe there is nothing more powerful than a man's hopes and expectations for tomorrow."

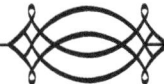

Sunset on the
Butler Chain of Lakes
Windemere, Fl

Mixed Media on Canvas, 30" x 24"

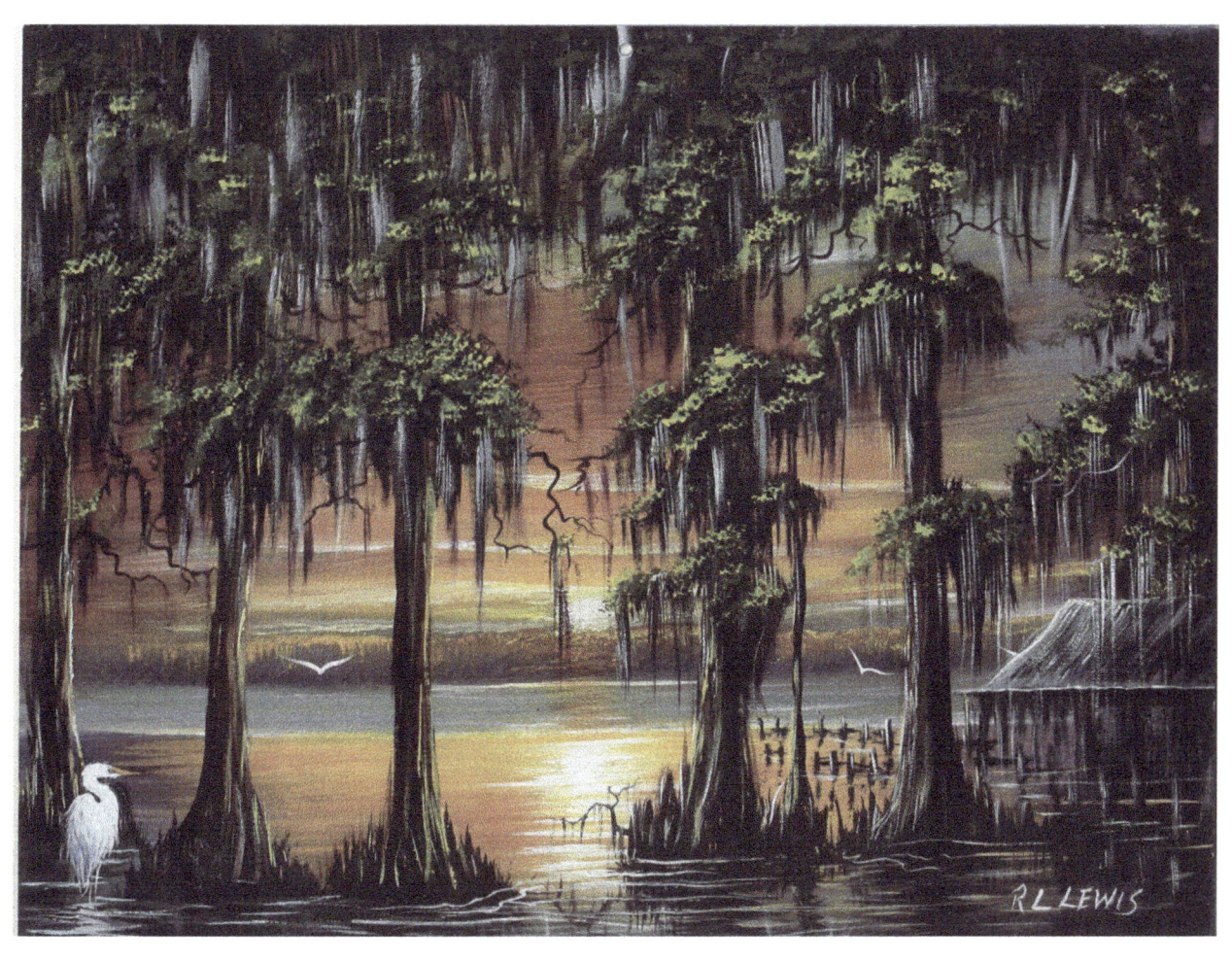

DID YOU KNOW:

*RL Lewis often enjoys painting
scenes from this river system.*

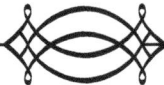

Multi-Hued Tomoka River
Ormond Beach, Fl

Mixed Media on Canvas, 30" x 24"

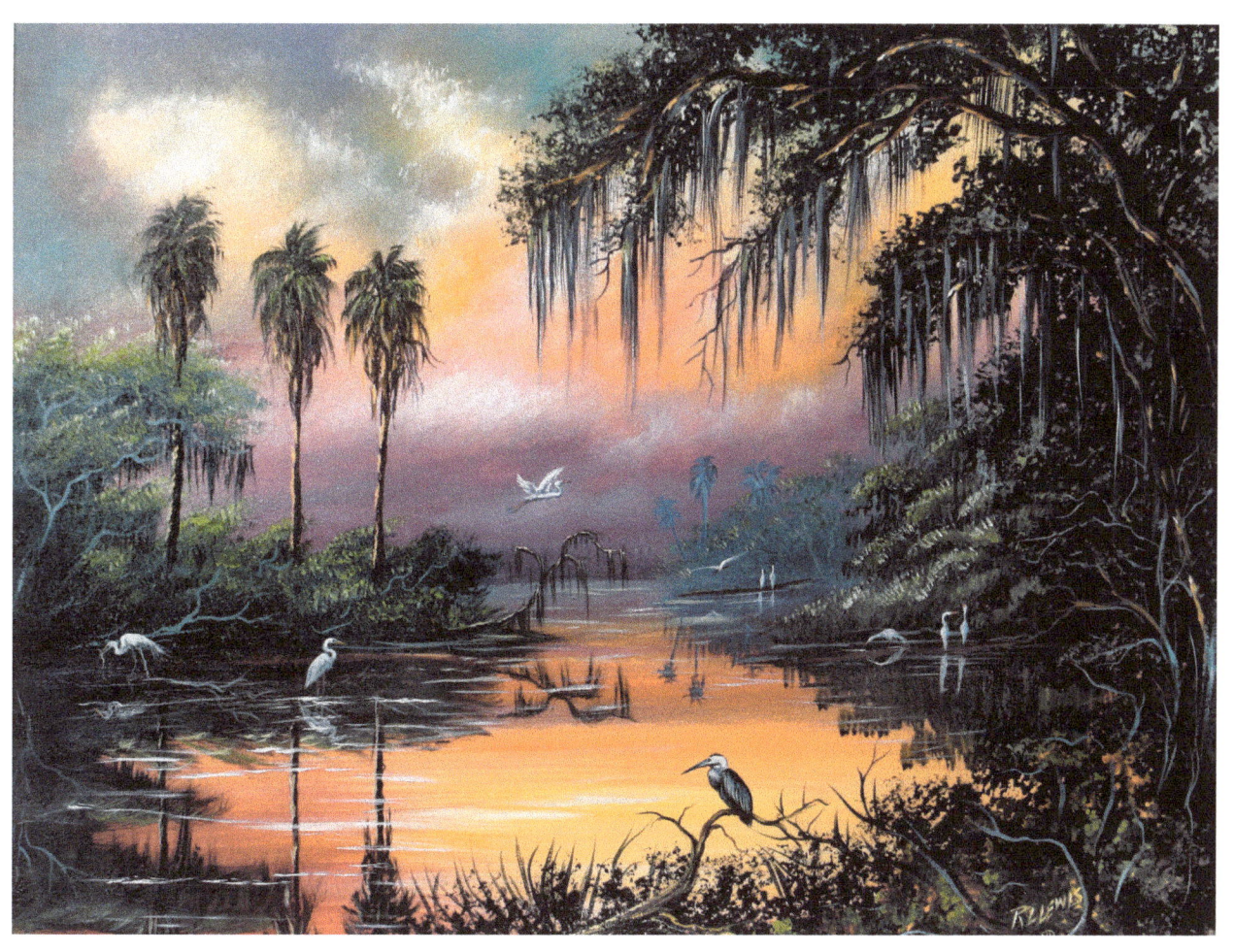

DID YOU KNOW:

The Tomoka River is also called the loop.

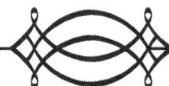

RL is very meticulous when painting beachside

waves and sea oats. He leans heavily on the palette

knife when painting these scenes.

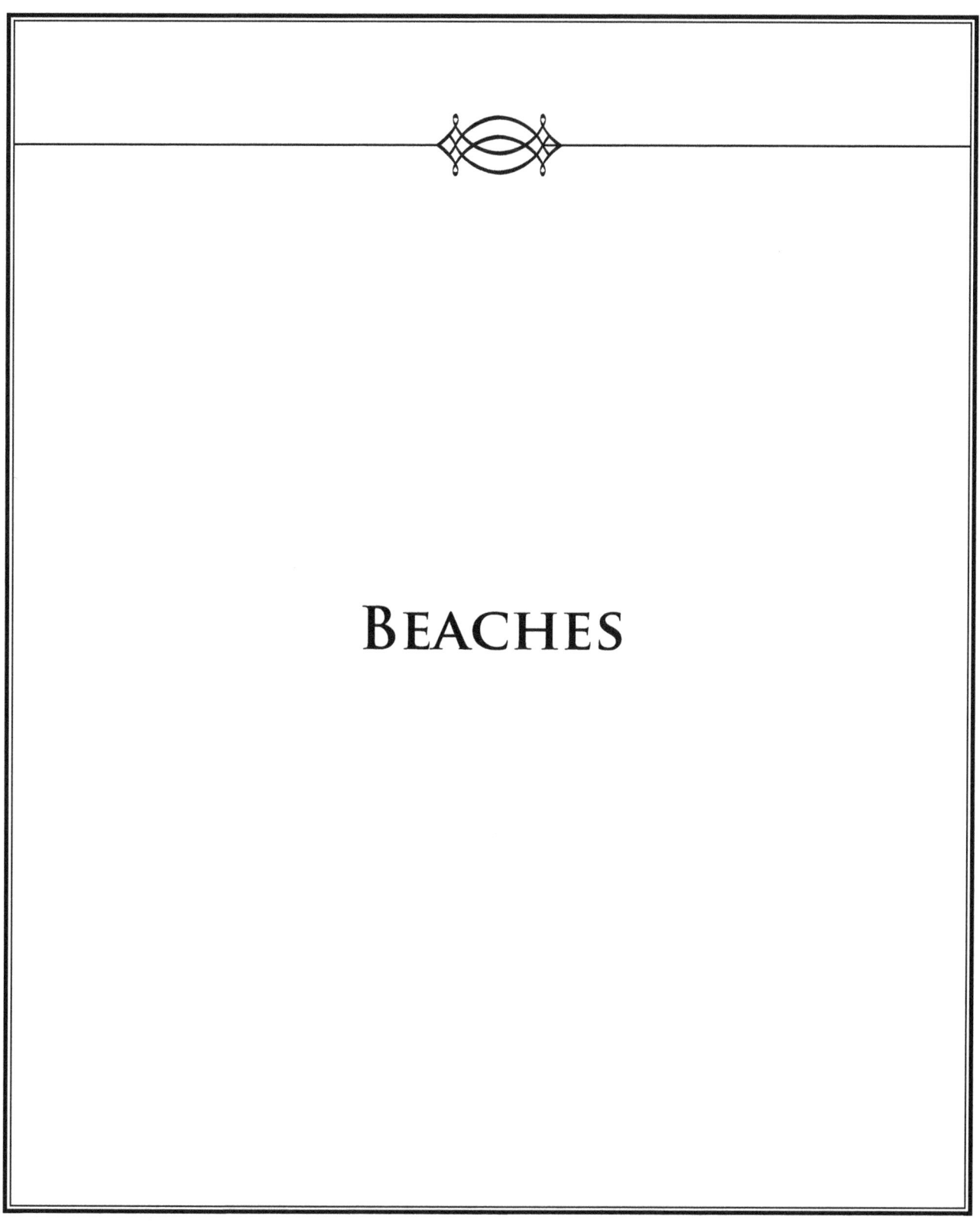

BEACHES

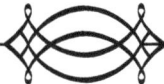

St. Joseph's Peninsula State Park
State Park
(St. Joe Bay and the Gulf of Mexico)
Port St. Joe, Fl

Acrylic on Canvas, 28" x 22"

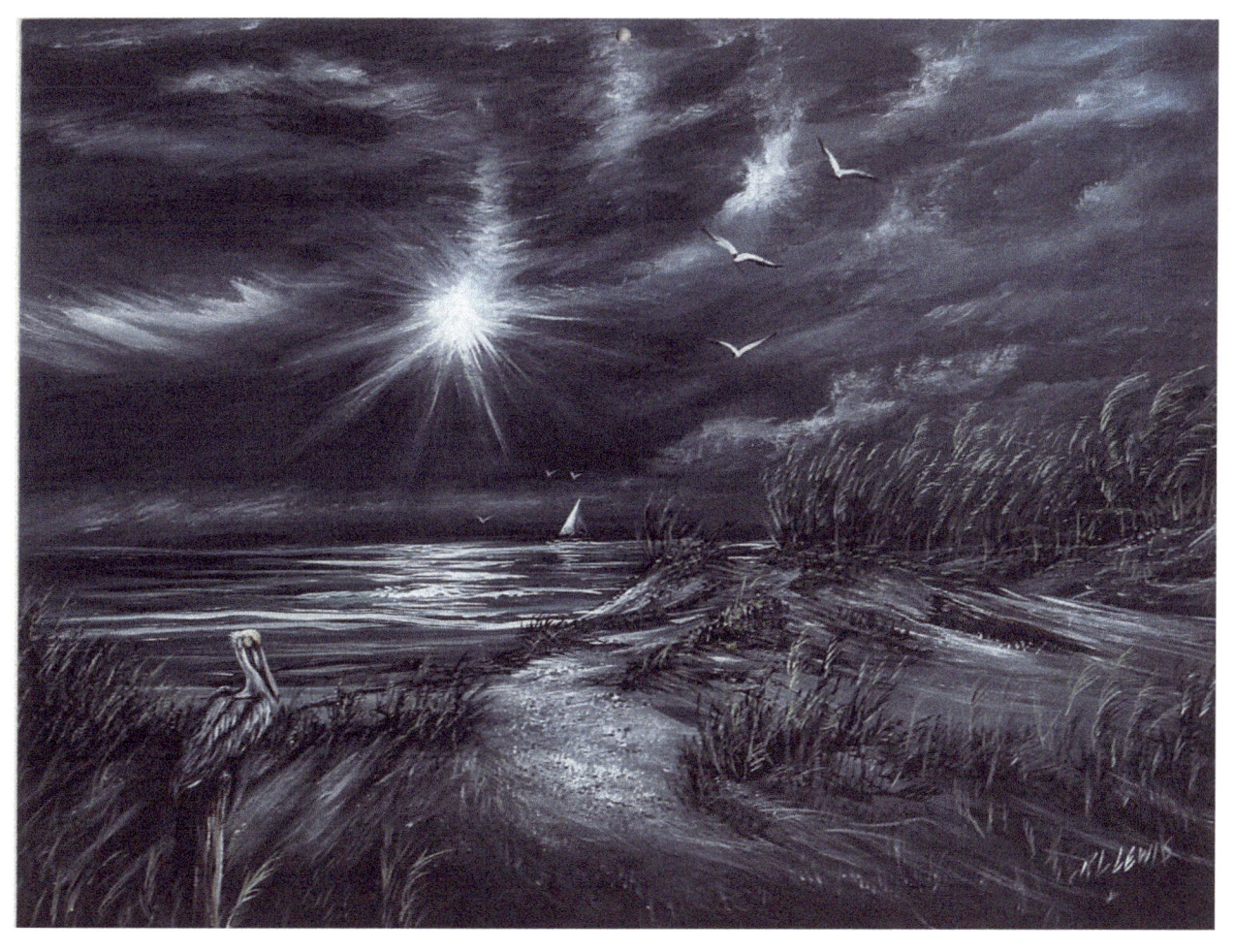

DID YOU KNOW:

This beach at one time was voted on of Florida's most beautiful beaches.

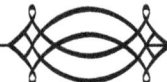

Cocoa Beach, Fl Sunrise
circa 1988

Oil on Canvas, 24" x 18"

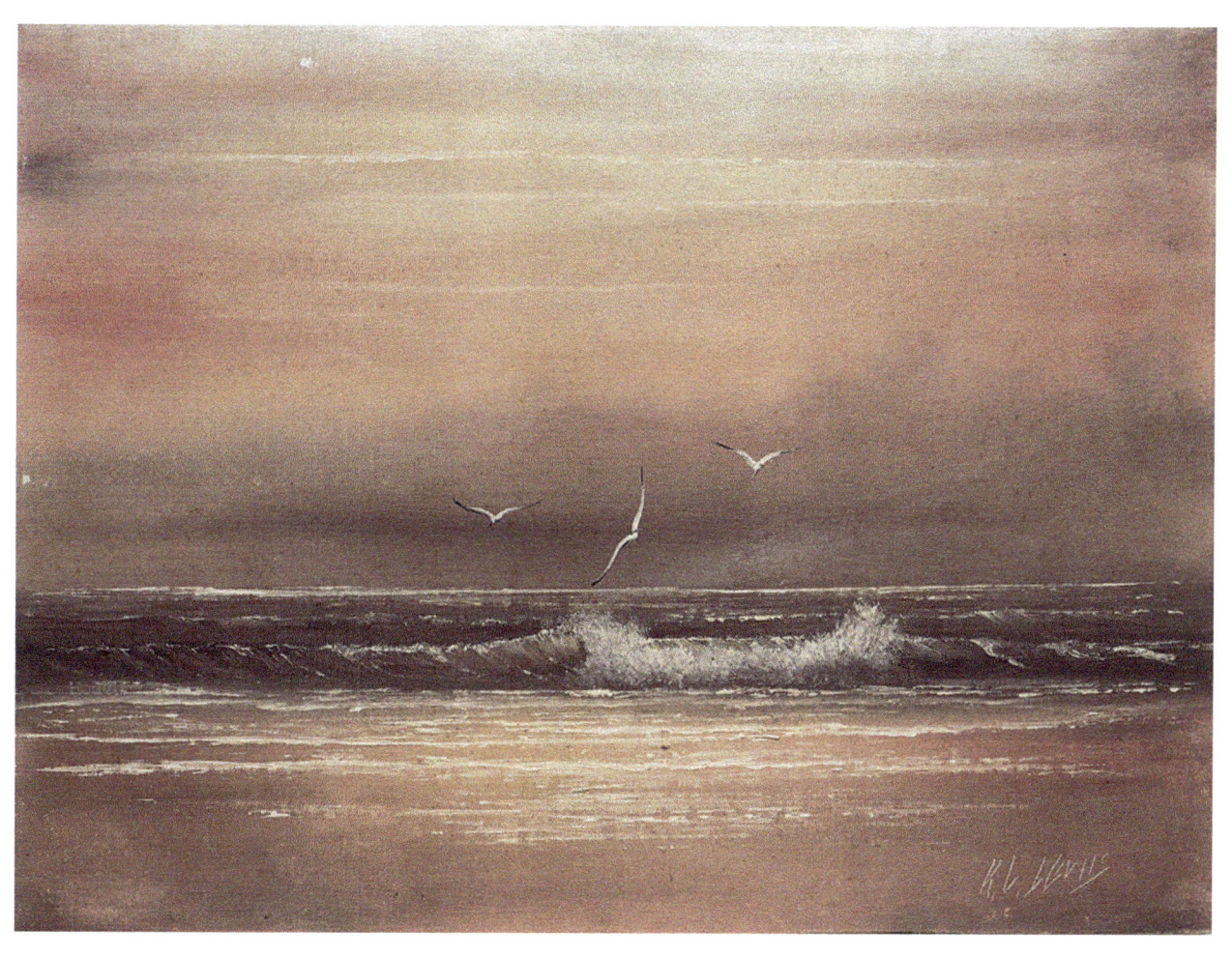

DID YOU KNOW:

Cocoa beach was one of RL's favorite places to sell paintings. It is also where he taught as a junior high teacher for twenty-two years.

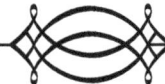

Spring Time on Jacksonville Beach, FL

Acrylic on Canvas 20" X 16"

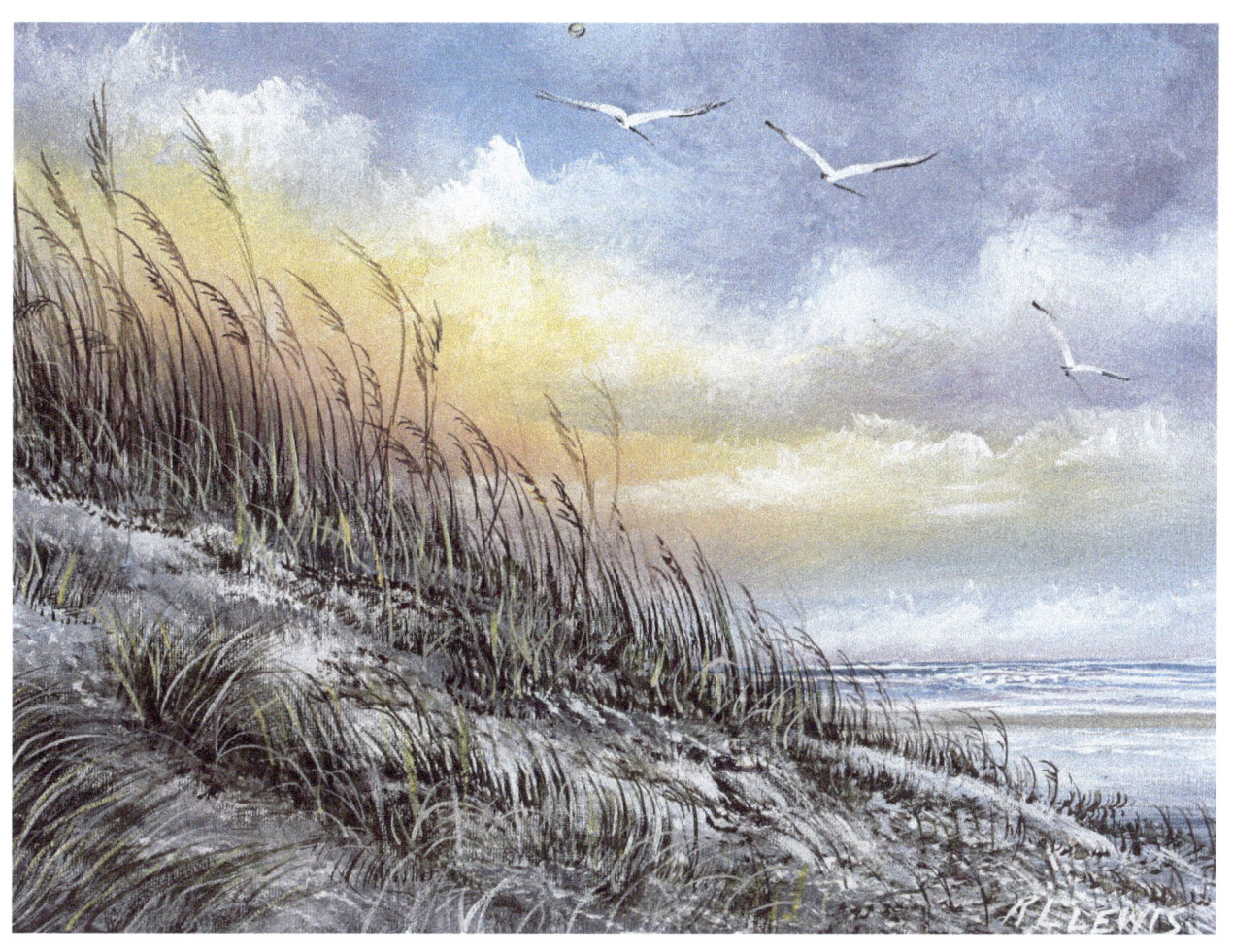

DID YOU KNOW:

RL Lewis painted this scene and three others, as part of the Jacksonville Beach Museum series sights and scenes.

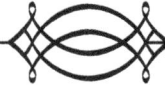

THE PICTURESQUE BEAUTY OF CEDAR KEY, FL CIRCA 1960S

Acrylic on Canvas 20" X 16"

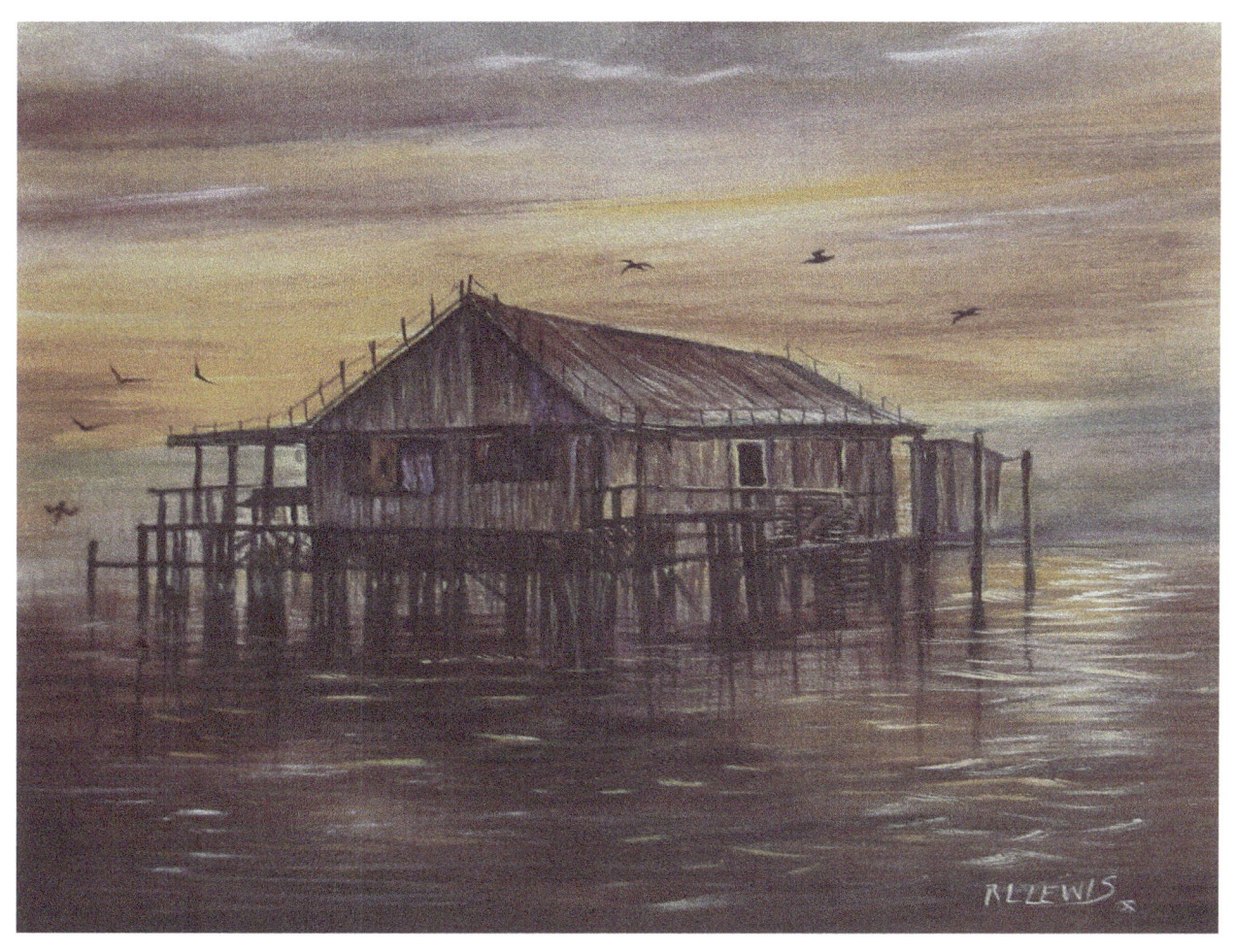

DID YOU KNOW:

The Thomas Guest House at Cedar Key is a small wooden cottage built on pilings. It was originally built in 1959.

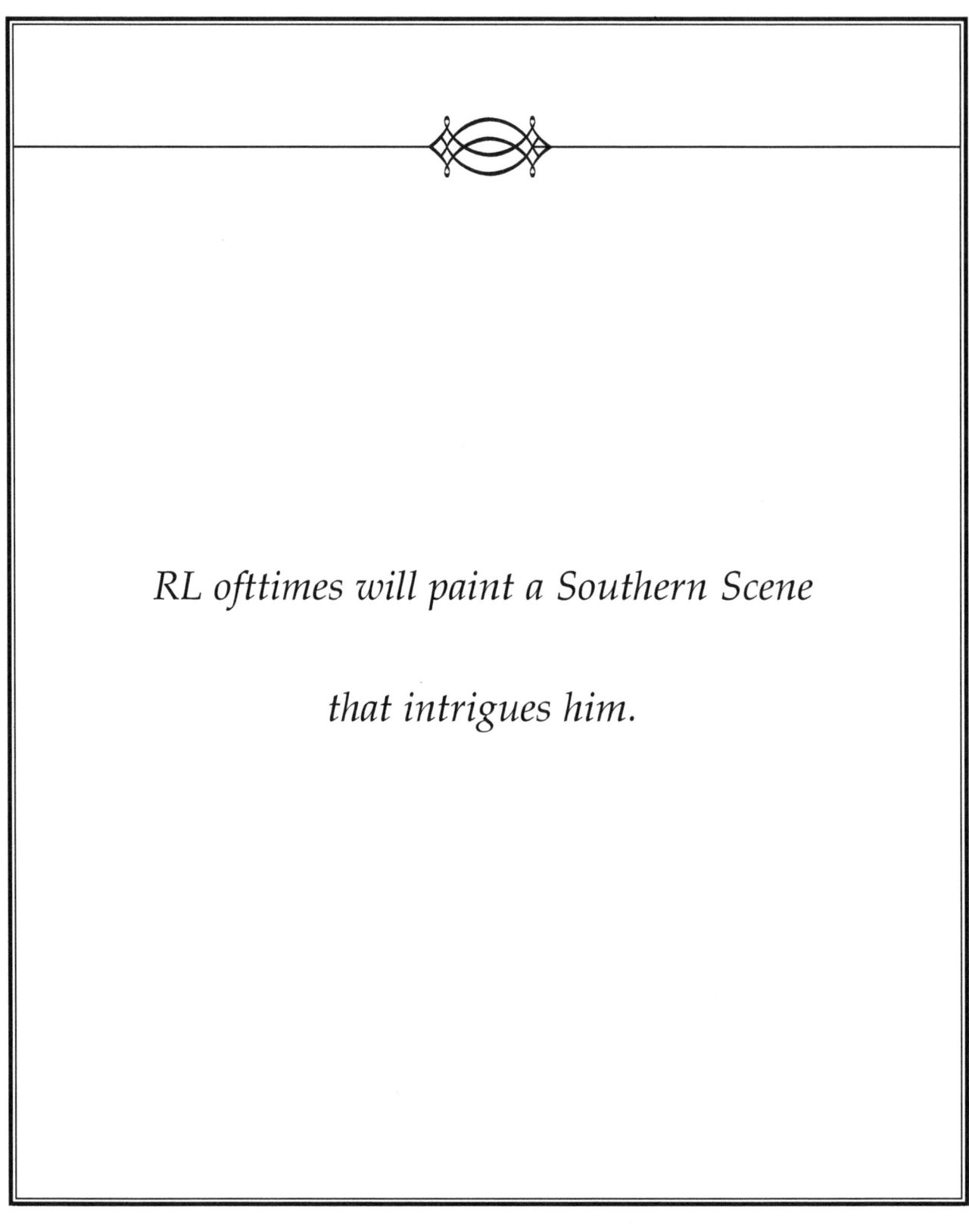

RL ofttimes will paint a Southern Scene

that intrigues him.

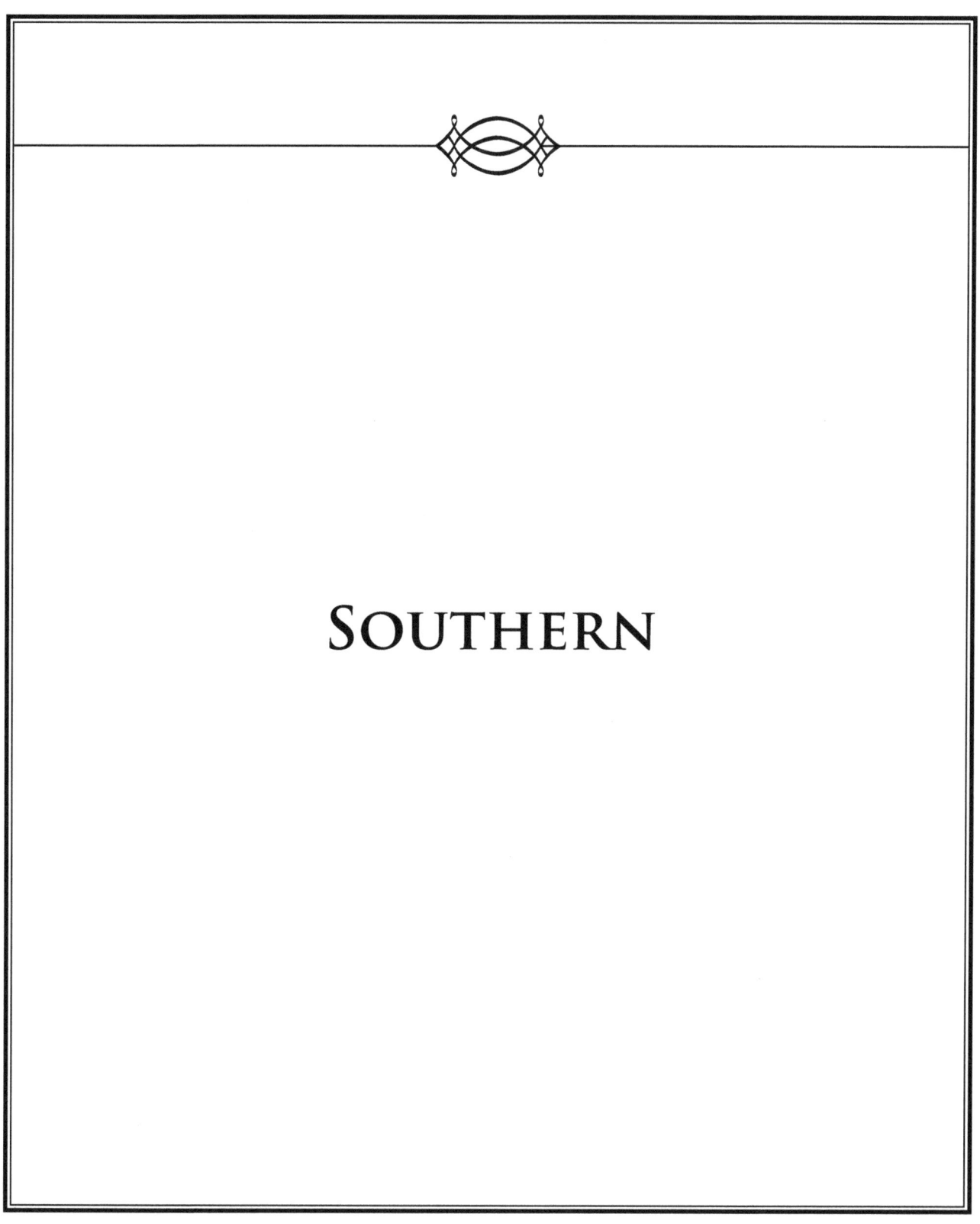

SOUTHERN

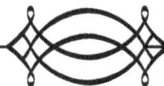

RABURN COUNTY MILL HOUSE, NORTHEAST GEORGIA FIVE MILES FROM THE NORTH CAROLINA SMOKY MOUNTAINS

Acrylic on Canvas, 30" x 24"

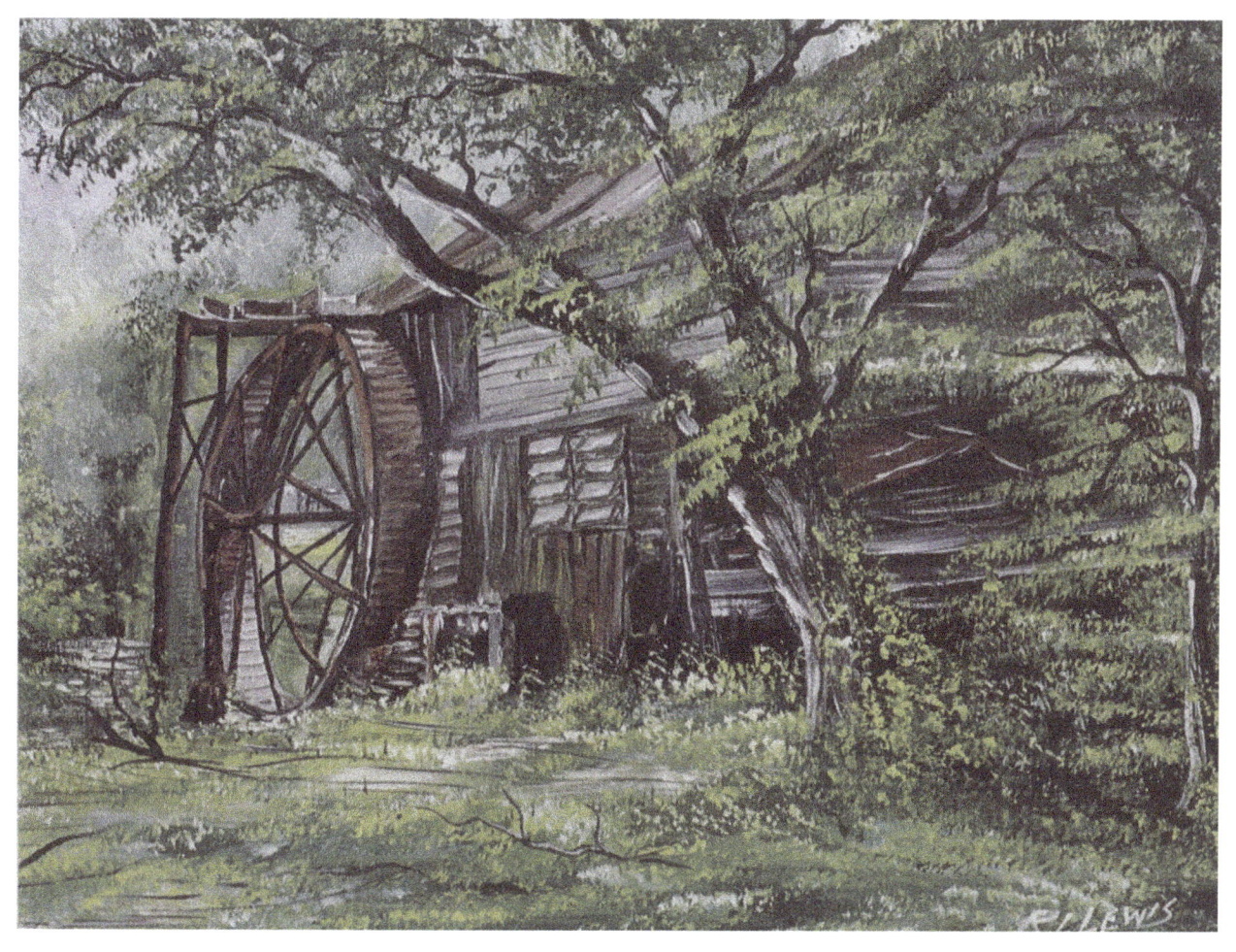

DID YOU KNOW:

RL enjoys the challenge of painting landscapes outside of his beloved Florida.

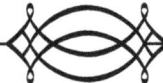

Be Careful Where You Settle
Okeefenokee Swamp
South Georgia

Acrylic on Canvas, 24" x 18"

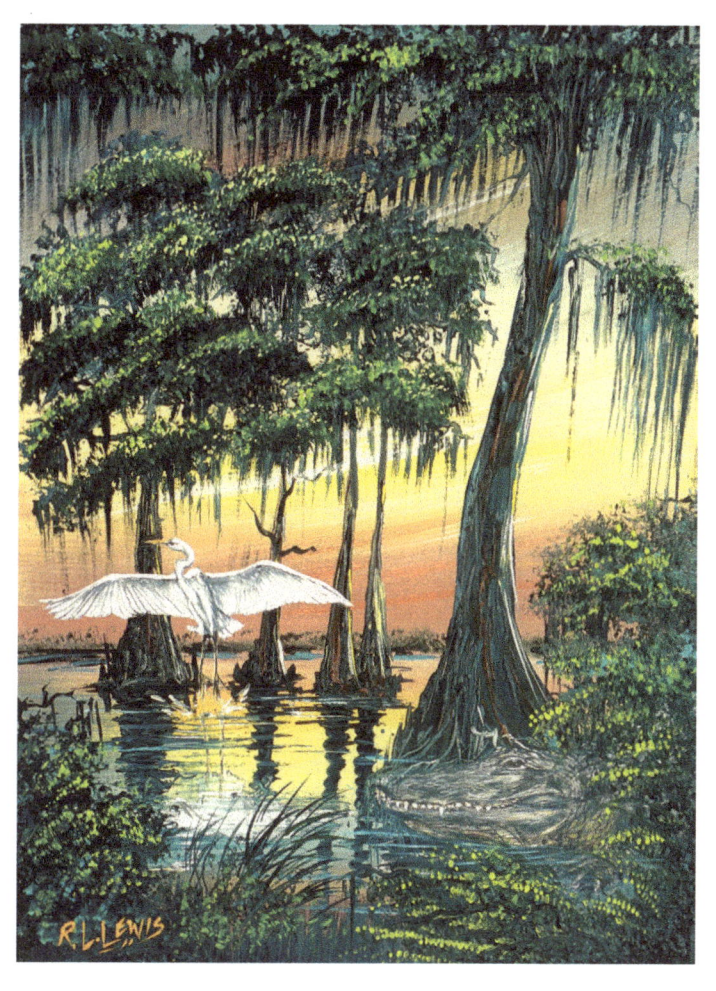

DID YOU KNOW:

RL enjoys painting deer, gator, cattle and various water fowl.

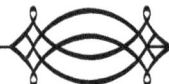

FALL IN VIRGINIA
CIRCA 1978

Oil on Canvas, 36″ x 24″

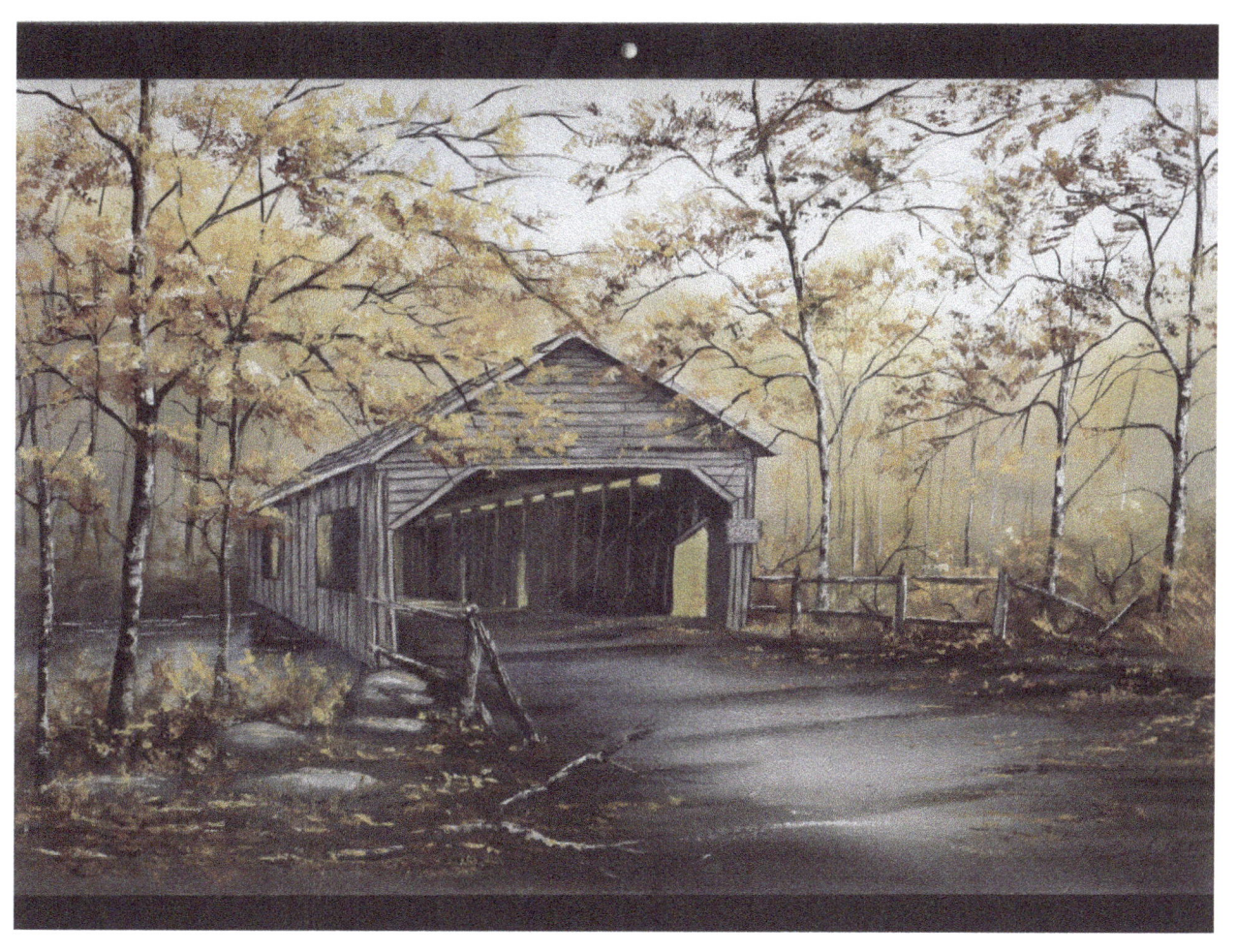

DID YOU KNOW:

This southern scene is one that Lewis purchased back from a collector because he simply loves this painting.

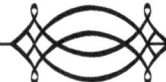

Manchac Swamp, New Orleans, La

Acrylic on Canvas, 30" x 24"

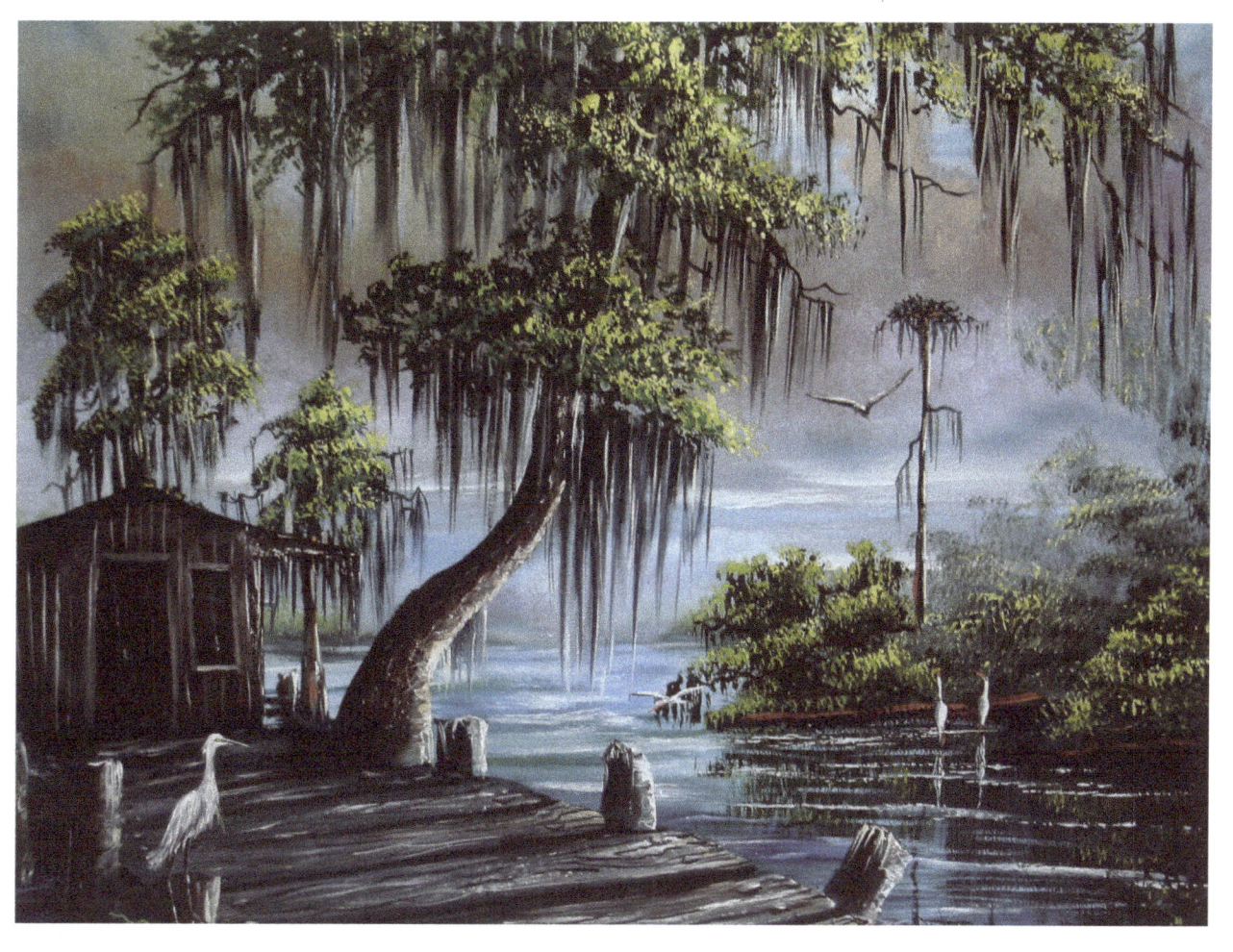

DID YOU KNOW:

RL's cypress swamp landscapes are known for its balance and mystique.

Contact the Author

Please email or write the author with any comments you may have. You are also welcome to contact him for bookings. Mr. Lewis is available for book club presentations, book signings, or speaking engagements for your organization.

Contact him at:

Email: rllewisartist@gmail.com

Phone: 321-543-1919

Visit our website at: www.rllewisartist.com

www.ingramcontent.com/pod-product-compliance
Lightning Source LLC
Chambersburg PA
CBHW052136170526
45162CB00003B/28